D0907669

Bicentennial Barns

OF OHIO

Copyright © 2003 by Christina Wilkinson
All rights reserved. This book may not
be reproduced, in whole or in part,
in any form without written permission
from the publisher.

Published by Rosewood Press
P.O. Box 1532
Mentor, Ohio 44061-1532

Designed by Mendelow + Johnson, Inc.
www.mendelow-johnson.com
Set in Mrs. Eaves and Charme

Edited by Nancy E. Piazza
Writeperson, Ltd.
www.writeperson.com

Printed in the United States of America
by Modern International Graphics, Inc.
Cleveland, Ohio

Officially licensed
by the Ohio Bicentennial Commission

Wilkinson, Christina
"Bicentennial Barns of Ohio"

Library of Congress Control Number: 2003094369

ISBN 0-9742020-0-2

Bicentennial Barns

OF OHIO

A tribute to the barns and their owners

BY Christina Wilkinson

Mentor, Ohio

www.rosewoodpress.com

A letter to the barn owners . . .

Dear Owners,

When I decided to do a book about Ohio's Bicentennial Barns, I knew I had to begin with you. Holding the optimistic view that some of you would consent to an in-person interview, I mailed eighty-eight letters of introduction and short questionnaires. Each afternoon, I approached the mailbox with great anticipation, hoping at least some of you would respond. For days there was nothing. And then they arrived: first from counties by the Ohio River, then from those in the northeast corner of the state, and soon from all regions of Ohio ★

Your responses exceeded my wildest expectations. Acting as ambassadors for your counties, you made time for me in your busy schedules and welcomed me into your homes. You gave me permission to wander around your properties, to make friends with your pets, inspect your barns, and greet your livestock. As the work on this book nears completion, I continue to be humbled by your warmth and hospitality ★

Time flew by as each of you shared your personal, and sometimes painful, memories and related stories of your past. I was invited to view family photograph albums, prized collections of antiques, family heirlooms, and restored classic cars and tractors. You trusted me, someone previously unknown to you, to sift through the information you provided, to print what was relevant, and protect the rest ★

What I deemed too personal to reveal, will be forever kept in my heart as treasured memories of the experience of a lifetime. I have done my best to tell your story as I heard it, using words both spoken and unspoken. I hope you feel the result is worthy of your faith in me. I thank you for the time and courtesy you have shown me, and in closing, it must be said that your importance to this project cannot be overlooked. For without you, there would be no Bicentennial Barns ★

Fondly,

Chris

About this book . . .

My introduction to Bicentennial Barns came in the spring of 2002. While writing for a small, local newspaper in my home state of Ohio, I was asked to cover the recently selected barn in Lake County. Barn owners Dan and Linda Hearn were on hand to welcome me into their home, and surrounded by their dogs, Cleo and Caesar, they told their story. Later we went outside, and Dan swung open the doors to the barn. Harboring a fondness for old buildings and interesting architecture, I was enchanted by the cathedral-like interior and massive beams ★

The Hearns' barn was dedicated at the end of June, and I returned to cover the celebration for the newspaper. I approached the Bicentennial Commission's Northeast Regional Coordinator, Jennifer Bucci, and asked if there was a book about the barns. No, she responded, but many people had asked for one. And that was the beginning ★

At Jennifer's suggestion, I adopted the project as my own. After securing licensing from the Bicentennial Commission, I mailed letters of introduction to the eighty-eight barn owners. I asked them to complete a brief questionnaire to facilitate what I was sure would become a daunting task of scheduling eighty-eight interviews in an orderly and logical sequence ★

With a swiftness that amazed me, the owners responded. Based upon their scheduling preferences, I divided the state into groups of seven to twelve counties. In the fall of 2002, I hit the road for the first time. Using Ohio's wonderful backbone of highways, I neared each region and then set off on rural back roads. During the next three months, I logged 7,400 miles, made seven multi-day trips, and fourteen one-day trips to visit each of the eighty-eight counties ★

The barn owners welcomed me into their homes and showered me with old-time country hospitality. They shared their stories, both funny and sad, and some memories that were too painful to be told without a tear. Together, we walked around their farms, while they tried to teach this city girl about hayforks, loose hay and baled hay, threshing floors, crop rotation, and livestock management ★

Through the present owners, I was introduced to some of the former owners of the farms, who reminisced about days gone by. They recounted what farming was like when real horsepower was used, followed by the increased use of steam-driven machinery. I heard stories of a simpler time, when people didn't have to have a drivers' license; as long as they could see over the wheel, they were good to go. Childhood memories of milk cans and threshing parties and hours spent playing in the barn. They were thrilled to be asked, happy that someone was interested ★

I knew going into this project that it would be a learning experience. As a seasoned traveler, I looked forward to seeing new areas of the state and visiting small towns with quaint village greens and crisp white bandstands. I met people who were genuine and sincere. They were real people who took the time to talk to me, offer advice, and give me shortcuts to my destinations. In many cases they simply suggested that I follow them as they led the way. I was touched by their warmth ★

The lessons learned on this journey will remain with me forever. Many of my relatives, ancestors who died long before I was born, were farmers. Although I never got to meet them face-to-face, I saw images of them, heard stories and descriptions, and in some cases, read their words. But not having been raised on a farm, I never really understood their lives ★

As I made my way through rural Ohio, I felt them reach out to me. And now I understand. I know how hard they worked, and how grateful they were for an occasional day of rest. Their lives began and ended on the farm; there was no time to travel, to see the rest of the world as I have done. There was only work: chores to be done, crops to be tended, livestock to be cared for. I thank them for their hard work and perseverance ★

The Bicentennial Barn-painting project pays tribute to all of Ohio's farmers, both past and present. With the hope of building a better life, early settlers loaded wagons and journeyed long distances to the new Ohio territory. They felled hundreds of trees, creating fields for crops and pastures for their animals. To shelter their families, they quickly constructed simple log cabins and then turned their attention to building the most important structure on their property: the barn ★

This project has truly been the experience of a lifetime for me, and I am profoundly grateful. I extend my thanks to the Bicentennial Commission, including Elizabeth Cobey-Piper and Lee Yochum, who believed I had the tenacity to complete the project, and to the barn owners for their hospitality. I also wish to express my gratitude to county historians, who took time to assist with my research. And not to be forgotten, special thanks to those citizens who saved me countless minutes and incalculable miles by happily saying, "Follow me!" as they led me down narrow country roads to my destination. May everyone enjoy reading this book as much as I have enjoyed writing it ★

About the barn painting project . . .

The success of the barn-painting project lies in its appeal to all generations. Everyone, it seems, is fascinated by the old, weathered structures that nestle in valleys or cling resolutely to hillsides. They tend to evoke a sense of nostalgia, a longing for simpler times. Bicentennial Barns symbolize the perseverance of Ohio's early residents, farmers who settled the Ohio territory 200 years ago ★

Hired by the Bicentennial Commission as the southeast regional coordinator, it was Nichola Moretti's job to acquaint people in her region about the upcoming Bicentennial celebration. As a child growing up in Meigs County, Nichola passed many barns as she traveled country roads with her family. Spotting barns was a way to make the time go faster, and they became landmarks of journeys frequently taken. Because of their sheer size, barns were often used to display advertising. It occurred to her that painting the Bicentennial logo on barns would effectively communicate her message to the public ★

Nichola searched in vain for a barn painter. It appeared to be a lost art. Then she entered the Barnesville Chamber of Commerce and happened upon a copy of the local newspaper, the Barnesville Enterprise. On the first page was a photograph of a barn painted with the logo of The Ohio State University Buckeyes. It was the creation of Scott Hagan, a young man from the nearby town of Jerusalem. Nichola Moretti knew she had found her barn painter ★

In the beginning, the idea was to paint only a few barns, but soon the project expanded to include a barn in each of Ohio's eighty-eight counties. Some barn owners offered their barns as soon as they heard about the project. Others barns were submitted by the public or suggested by the regional coordinators. The decision was based on the condition of the wood, the direction the barn faced, and its location, preferably on a heavily traveled state route. In some counties it was difficult to find the ideal barn, but before the project was over, more than 2,000 people across the state had volunteered their barns ★

While it is undisputed that Nichola Moretti developed the project, Scott Hagan turned it into a reality. Only age twenty-two when he began, he completed eighty-eight barns in five years and put 65,000 miles on his truck. In 1998, the first barn painting took place in Belmont County, where Scott lived. He painted without an audience, and only a few attended the dedication ceremony. It was just the beginning ★

Using only Sherwin Williams paint, Scott painted logos on twelve barns that first year. He perfected the use of the scaffolding system and improved his painting technique. In 1999, he painted twenty barns, and people began to notice. By the millennium year, he really hit his stride. His schedule for twenty-one barns was published, and people arrived on the first day of painting. As he threw up his scaffolding, they set up their lawn chairs. With rapt attention, they watched as he tuned his radio to listen to a ball game and hoisted himself into position. Before their eyes, the twenty-by-twenty-foot logo took shape, as Scott sketched it freehand with painters' chalk. Once satisfied, the artist began to paint ★

The logos took approximately eighteen hours and seven gallons of paint. Some barns took a bit longer, especially those with tongue and groove siding. Some very weathered barns took over twenty gallons of paint. In the end, the project consumed 645 gallons of paint; there were thirty red barns, fifty-four white, four brown, and one yellow. Early barns showed the logo painted over the outline of the state; in later versions he eliminated the state. Scott was creative in his approach and tried to make each barn distinctive by details such as stars or special shading. All barns bear his signature in the lower right hand corner, along with the sequence in which they were painted ★

By 2002, Scott Hagan had a following, barn groupies as they were called. Many had been to every barn and carried scrapbooks of photographs and newspaper articles. Armed with cameras, motorcycle clubs and car enthusiasts held rallies. Schoolchildren took field trips to the barns to learn about local history and have their class picture taken in front of them.

Barn owners were staggered at the volume of people who came to view and photograph their barns. No one could have predicted it ★

The enthusiasm displayed by the public caught everyone by surprise, but the project came at a time when Americans everywhere were wearing their patriotic hearts on their sleeves. Security issues caused people travel concerns, but they still had vacation time. Instead of taking long, expensive trips, they piled the family into the car and went in search of the barns with the distinctive red, white, and blue logo. The Bicentennial Barns became not only a symbol of Ohio's 200th birthday, but a tribute to our early settlers, patriotic pioneers of a new country who carved a state out of the wilderness that was Ohio ★

A note about Scott...

Courtesy of Ohio Bicentennial Commission.

It all began in October of 1997, when twenty-one-year-old Scott Hagan painted The Ohio State University Buckeye logo on his father's barn. His late grandfather liked it so much that he snapped a photograph and sent it to the local newspaper, the Barnesville Enterprise. The family was thrilled when it appeared on the front page, never imagining that a grandfather's pride would launch Scott into a new career. Soon his artwork would appear on front pages all over Ohio ★

Scott Hagan grew up in the small town of Jerusalem, in Belmont County. The Hagan farm was just twenty minutes away from the home of Harley Warrick, the painter who covered the side of many a barn with the Mail Pouch Tobacco advertisement. In his youth, Scott never had the opportunity to meet the painter. Later, Harley would play an important role in Scott's life. When Scott graduated from high school, his mother prayed that he would find a job doing what he loved. And what he loved was art ★

Bicentennial Southeast Regional Coordinator Nichola Moretti saw a copy of the Barnesville Enterprise and knew that Scott Hagan was the person she had been looking for. No one was more surprised than the artist when he received that first telephone call. A series of calls followed, including a visit to Columbus. In the end, they convinced him. Scott Hagan signed a contract with the Bicentennial Commission to paint the official logo on a few barns. With the stroke of a pen, the barn-painting project was born ★

To prepare for his new job, Scott introduced himself to Harley Warrick. Harley graciously showed him how to rig scaffolding with a rope and pulley system. The two men became good friends and enjoyed sharing barn-painting stories. Harley Warrick passed away in November of 2000 and Scott greatly misses him. Scott still stands on a plank, or "pick," the painter gave him ★

The first Bicentennial Barn was painted in the spring of 1998, in Scott's home county of Belmont. It didn't create much of a stir; few people even noticed, and the dedication was a small event. Ohio's 200th birthday was still four years away ★

Scott Hagan officially painted his last barn in September of 2002. By then he had become a celebrity. His fans were legion; they followed him from county to county, barn to barn. It was not just his talent that made Scott such a success. He was, and continues to be, quiet, soft-spoken, and unfailingly polite. The quintessential American young man, raised on a farm in small-town Ohio. The Bicentennial Commission could not have made a better choice ★

Recently married, Scott and his wife, Amanda, continue to live in Belmont County. He now has his own business and a Web site. Scott can be hired to paint logos of all sorts, as well as farm names and patriotic themes. In 2003, Scott Hagan will continue to be available to fill requests made by the Bicentennial Commission for additional painting and personal appearances. As this project draws to a close, he is hopeful new artistic opportunities will come his way. Scott Hagan can be reached at: www.barnartist.com ★

Bicentennial Barns

OF OHIO

Adams

OWNER
Jean and Charles Kirker Jr.

LOCATION
6620 State Route 136, in West Union

Kirkwood Farm sits on the crest of a hill, near the town of West Union. Surrounded by acres of farmland, the picturesque setting includes two barns and a honey-colored stone house. The present owner, Charles Kirker, was born in the house and is the fifth generation to live in the homestead. Owner of the Adams County Bicentennial Barn, he didn't need a logo on his barn to prompt him to think about the history of his farm. He lives it everyday of his life ★

The farm has been in the Kirker family since Thomas Kirker moved to Ohio in 1790. Kirker, who served two terms as the second Governor of Ohio, helped to name and design the town of West Union in 1804. A year later, he began to build a house on his farm, southwest of the city ★

The Kirker home was constructed by stonemason Thomas Metcalf, using sandstone from the property. Metcalf, who also built the Presbyterian Church in West Union, went on to become the Governor of Kentucky. The Kirkers raised thirteen children in the small house. Their youngest son, George, inherited the property upon his father's death in 1837 ★

George Kirker, perhaps remembering how cramped the house had been when he was growing up, built an addition in 1858. His next project was to construct a large bank barn to accommodate the herd of Shorthorn Cattle he had imported from Scotland. But the Civil War interfered with his plans. George was elected captain of the 141st Ohio Volunteer Infantry, and duty to his country delayed work on the barn ★

The Civil War touched the community in many ways. Metcalf's Presbyterian church, referred to as the church of governors, was used as a barracks for Union soldiers. The people of West Union, located about ten miles from the Ohio River, were sympathetic to slaves escaping from the south, and Captain Kirker's farmhouse became a stop on the Underground Railroad. When Morgan's Raiders infiltrated Ohio, word traveled quickly. Members of the Kirker clan fled to the woods with the horses to prevent them from being used in the Confederate Army ★

The barn construction, begun in 1861, was finally completed in 1862. Timber for the framing of the forty-by-eighty-foot barn was cut on the property. The siding was made from Pennsylvania Pine, rafted down the Ohio River. For many years the barn sheltered cattle. Shorthorn cattle are still raised at Kirkwood Farm, but the barn is now primarily used for storage of hay and straw ★

Charles and Jean Kirker continue to occupy the original homestead. They renovated it in 1972, retaining the charm of earlier years. Photographs of Kirker ancestors line the walls of a small study, while the main living area displays colorful images of their three children along with their grandchildren. The Kirkers are understandably proud of their ancestors, many of whom are buried in the cemetery across the street. They hope future generations will preserve the homestead and continue to maintain the historic Adams County Bicentennial Barn ★

Allen

OWNER
Allen County Commissioners

LOCATION
1582 Slabtown Road, in Lima

A white picket fence extends along State Route 81 leading to the entrance of the Allen County Farm Park, with its large red and white Bicentennial Barn. One of ten parks managed by the Johnny Appleseed Metropolitan Park District, the grounds were once part of the Allen County Infirmary and Children's Home ★

County homes, referred to as homes for the infirm, were built to house residents of the county unable to live independently. Allen County's complex included over 300 acres of buildings and farmland. Able-bodied residents helped on the farm by tending the animals and working in the gardens. They raised hogs and cattle, kept a flock of turkeys, and had a large chicken coop. All meat and vegetables consumed were grown on the property ★

In 1978, the Metropolitan Park District approached the Commissioners about leasing land and buildings for a farm park. An agreement was formalized in 1982, providing use of forty-five acres through the year 2071, at no cost to the park district. The property included the two large barns and several outbuildings, all painted white with black trim ★

The barns had not been used for livestock for at least ten years. Everything was left in place, as though waiting for the animals to return, and park employees worked long hours removing hay and straw. The Bicentennial Barn was the cattle barn, and measures forty by eighty feet. Designed as a bank barn, the animals and dairy were located on the lower level with storage above. Built over a hundred years ago, the timbers used in the construction came from huge trees on the property ★

The original home, no longer standing, was built in 1856. A rebuilt version of the home is located adjacent to the Farm Park, as is the Allen County Children's Home. Ottawa Metro Park and McLean-Teddy Bear Park are on approximately 145 acres that were also part of the original farm ★

Courtesy of Allen County Farm Park.

With buildings repaired and repainted bright red, the Allen County Farm Park now hosts annual events which focus on pioneer-era farming activities. Visitors can experience horse-drawn hayrides, watch threshing demonstrations, and enjoy cider made on-site from an old press. Animals are not kept permanently on the grounds but are brought in for appropriate functions. The Johnny Appleseed Park District is committed to both preservation and education. It has found a way to combine both in the Allen County Farm Park and is proud the barn was chosen to represent the county for Ohio's Bicentennial celebration ★

Ashland

OWNER
Mark and Cheryl Smith

LOCATION
974 County Road 1600, in Ashland

Visitors traveling north on Ohio's Interstate 71 are welcomed to Ashland County by Mark and Cheryl Smith's Bicentennial Barn. The hundred-year-old barn once towered over many acres of pasture and farmland. The farm is smaller now, and cattle are no longer grazing on the hillside, but the barn is still a picturesque reminder of rural Ohio ★

An 1861 map of Ashland County indicates that at the start of the Civil War, P. Thomas owned a large farm, including the land the Smiths now own. The farm was sold to George Smith in 1874. His heirs sold the farm at a Sheriff's sale in 1918. George W. Schuck was the winning bidder of the ninety-five-acre farm. He later divided the farm, selling the eastern half ★

During the 1930s, the property had a succession of owners. In September of 1940, Irvin and Lela Landis purchased the farm, listed as forty-five and one half acres. Their three children: Jim, Nancy, and Betty grew up there. At least fifteen head of dairy cattle occupied the barn, all milked by hand in stanchions built over a cement floor ★

In 1958, Interstate 71 divided the farm. Landis sold it in May of 1959 to Clarence Young. On September 27, 1985, Larry and Darcus Duley bought the farm from Young. In 1991,they sold it to Mark and Cheryl Smith ★

The Smiths grow corn and soybeans on their acreage. The barn, built in the early 1900s, is used to store hay and straw. Scott Hagan tried not to have all the logos look exactly alike; he added shading to the Smiths' barn to give it a very distinctive look. Mark and Cheryl are proud to be the owners of the Ashland County Bicentennial Barn ★

Ashtabula

OWNER
Leta Divine

LOCATION
1648 Overly Road, in Jefferson

In 1914, when Clarence Guy Divine acquired the circa-1885 house and barn on the outskirts of Jefferson, the state of Ohio was only III years old. He could never have imagined that one day his former dairy barn would be chosen to represent Ashtabula County as part of the state's 200th birthday celebration ★

His son Charles was four years old when the family moved onto the farm. He remained there, running the dairy farm that his father started during the Depression. After World War II, Charles continued farming but also worked construction to make ends meet. He gradually sold off all the animals, and eventually the barn was used only for storage ★

Charles' sister, Nellie Divine McCoy, grew up on the farm, too. She has fond memories of their mother, Ollie, playing piano, with the family gathered 'round to sing. Nellie remembers watching her father and brothers milk the cows by hand. Clarence Divine refused to teach his daughter to milk for fear she would marry a man who would put her to work. Nellie has memories of her father and his hired hands carting at least ten of the ten-gallon milk cans down to the milk stand set up near the road. Each day a truck would pick them up and deliver them to a dairy in Dorset ★

Nellie walked to a small one-room schoolhouse a quarter mile down the road. There, a teacher, who boarded with area families, taught grades one through eight. After graduating the tiny school in 1927, Nellie rode with a friend to Jefferson High School to attend the ninth grade. During grades ten through twelve, she lived with a family in town, taking care of their children in exchange for room and board. On the weekends she returned home to the farm ★

Charles' wife, Leta, wanted to retain the property after her husband's death in 1976, and she asked their son Roger and his wife, Marsha, to move in with her and manage the farm. Roger and Marsha have lived there ever since, raising their own family and now helping to care for Leta, whose health isn't quite what it used to be ★

Roger has made several changes, but his ancestors would still recognize their homestead. To store his tractor and other equipment, Roger constructed a pole barn and returned cattle to the old barn, believing that a structure is best used for its intended purpose. An addition was put on the barn not long after the logo was painted. Although changes to the interior have been made over the years, the rear of the barn is original to the 1930s, as Roger remembers it in his grandfather's day. Currently forty-five head of beef cattle call the barn home ★

The Divines are amazed at the interest the barn has generated. Since it was selected by the Bicentennial Commission, they have collected newspaper articles, photos, and other memorabilia to remind them of the experience. They are particularly proud of a letter signed by Governor Bob Taft, praising the quality of the homegrown beef in the hamburgers he ate at their home. Taft and his wife, Hope, were in the area to attend a nearby covered bridge festival and hopped on their bikes to see the Divines' barn ★

Roger, Marsha, and Leta are delighted that their barn was selected to represent Ashtabula County. Their three grandchildren love spending time on the farm, and Roger hopes that one of them will carry on the family tradition of farming that his grandfather started when he purchased the property so many years ago. In the meantime, he will continue to maintain the house and barn, so that future generations may enjoy it ★

Athens

OWNER
Mary Ellen Hanning

LOCATION
3780 Enlow Road, in Athens

In the early 1900s, Cydnor Riley purchased acreage on Enlow Road, near the city of Athens. The tidy farm complex, with white house and barn, sat close to the road, surrounded by acres of crops and grazing cattle. There, he began the prosperous dairy business he would operate for the rest of his life ★

The Rileys raised their family in the farmhouse believed to have been part of the Underground Railroad. Daughter Mary Ellen grew up there and continues to call it home. She fondly remembers the days when cattle and horses lived in the barn, and the haymow was always filled. It was a time of milk cans and cream separators and just plain hard work ★

The Rileys had regular customers who came to them for their dairy products; no one went to a store for milk. The family also raised chickens, which were kept on the second level of the barn, and had a huge vegetable garden. The farm bustled in those days, and everyone pitched in to help. Mary Ellen and her sister had chores to do after school, both inside and out ★

Cydnor Riley saw many changes in his lifetime. When he bought the farm, Enlow Road was a narrow lane running in front of his barn and farmhouse, and he owned the acreage on both sides. Cydnor and his family could sit on the wide front porch, chatting with each other as they looked out across their fields. Back then, it was possible to hold a conversation on the porch. He would never have believed that a new road, State Route 50, would bring thousands of vehicles per day past his home. The view from the porch is no longer peaceful, and conversation is out of the question, drowned out by the whine of eighteen-wheelers ★

The Riley daughters inherited the farm after the death of their parents. In 1976, Mary Ellen and her husband, Kermit Hanning, bought her sister's share of the property. A few years later, the Hannings sold the land across the highway from the house and barn. Both structures continue to be lovingly preserved. The barn is unchanged, although no longer used for livestock. Repairs are made as necessary; new windows have been installed throughout ★

Recently widowed, Mary Ellen continues to maintain her property with help from her son, Tim, who lives nearby. A farmer's daughter and farmer's wife, she is a no-nonsense, do-what-has-to-be-done kind of person. Over the years, she learned how to make do and prepare for potential lean times. Her basement is testimony to that, as rows of shelves are lined with cans of vegetables and meat that she has put away for winter. Determined to stay active, she still works in her garden and digs out potatoes by herself ★

When the Bicentennial logo was painted on her barn, no one, except for Cydnor Riley, could have been prouder. Seen from the highway, the little farm is a tranquil scene of days gone by, simpler and quieter times, when milk cans were lined up next to the barn, and cows could be seen from the windows of the farmhouse. Mary Ellen is committed to preserving that memory for the next generation to enjoy ★

Auglaize

OWNER
Alice Jeannette Heckman

LOCATION
Interstate 75N, north of Wapakoneta

Auglaize County was formed in 1848 and named for the Auglaize River, which meanders through it. The river's banks were prime hunting ground for the Shawnee Indians who first settled Wapakoneta, now the county seat. During summers spent on her father's farm, Alice Jeannette Heckman remembers the riverbank as prime ground for picnicking. The river was a short pony ride from the farm and a cool escape from hot Ohio summers. It is Heckman's farm now, and she is honored to have it represent Auglaize County ★

Heckman's father, Carl F. Wintzer, purchased the farm in the early 1930s. Wintzer rented the farmhouse to tenant farmer Hugo Berg, who had two sons, Jack and Joe. The boys were close in age to Heckman's brother, Fred, and the children all became good friends. Fred remembers picking tomatoes in the blazing August sun; there were always a few tomato fights. Afterward, they went to a favorite swimming hole to cool off ★

The house and land continue to be used as rental property. Heckman doesn't know when her barn was built, but it was before her father purchased the farm. After her barn was selected as the Bicentennial Barn, Heckman repaired the siding and gave it a new coat of paint. It was ready and waiting for Scott Hagan when he arrived. Alice Jeannette Heckman is proud to own the Auglaize County barn and is looking forward to celebrating the Bicentennial in 2003 ★

Belmont

OWNER
Roger and Cathy Perkins

LOCATION
State Route 149, in Morristown

In 1998, a young man entered the office of Classic A Properties to ask Roger and Cathy Perkins about the white barn next door. He said his name was Scott Hagan, and he lived in the Belmont County town of Jerusalem. To their surprise, Scott offered to paint one end of the barn for free. There was a stipulation: It would be adorned with the State of Ohio's Bicentennial logo. Roger and Cathy agreed, and the Belmont County barn became the first of eighty-eight to be painted ★

Roger and Cathy Perkins purchased the former dairy barn, along with a house and sixty-five acres of property, from the Dunlap family in 1988. They know the Palmers owned the farm around 1900, but are unsure how large it may have been or when the barn was built. Roger and Cathy use their acreage for the production of hay and keep equipment in the barn ★

The dedication ceremony was small, attended by very few people. Although the event was well publicized, the painting of a barn, in this largely rural county, did not create much of a stir. In 2000, Scott returned to the Perkinses farm to repaint the faded logo. By then he was well-known as the official Bicentennial Barn painter and had acquired a large following ★

Roger and Cathy Perkins are proud to have been there from the beginning of Ohio's Bicentennial Barn-painting project. The Perkinses agree that they never anticipated the enthusiasm the public would display for the old structures. They are delighted with Scott Hagan's success and enjoy owning the barn that started it all, the Belmont County Bicentennial Barn ★

Brown

OWNER
Bob and Carol Groh

LOCATION
State Route 52, in Ripley

The historic town of Ripley is perched on the banks of the Ohio River. The riverfront is lined with stately homes, many of which were stops on the Underground Railroad. Harriet Beecher Stowe was told the story of a slave who escaped across the river to the shores of Ripley. She later included the account in her novel *Uncle Tom's Cabin*. Brown County's most important cash crop is tobacco, and Ohio's only tobacco market is located in Ripley. Appropriately, the structure chosen as Brown County's Bicentennial Barn, is a little brown tobacco barn, belonging to Bob and Carol Groh and their son, Andrew ★

For Bob Groh, buying the tobacco farm seemed like he was finally coming home. He was born in the tidy farmhouse his father rented, and the family lived there for several years before moving on. Even though he no longer rented the home, Bob's father continued to farm the land, so they were never far away. Bob was too small to remember when Ohio built Route 52, but his father often told him about moving the barn ★

The barn was used to dry and store the tobacco grown on the fifty-plus-acre farm. As plans for the road were designed, it became obvious that the barn was going to be in the middle of the proposed construction. Built in the late 1800s, the barn was supported with twelve-by-twelve-inch, hand-hewn sills. Determined to keep the barn, the owner jacked it up under the sills and rolled it to its present location ★

When Bob and Carol purchased the farm in 1974, there were only twenty-two acres left. Because it was so visible from the road, the barn became the perfect billboard. Both the roof and the side of the barn bore advertising logos. The roof sign proclaimed, "See Seven States From Rock City," and the side of the barn was adorned with a sign for Bavarian Beer. The Grohs replaced much of the siding and added a shed for additional storage. In 1993, a new, standing-seam roof was installed out of necessity. A small tornado touched down, ripping off the old roof and causing damage to the farmhouse ★

Bob and his son, Andrew, grow tobacco and corn on the farm and use the barn for its intended purpose. The barn also provides shelter for their chickens, an unrestored '55 Chevy, and a 1923 Fordson tractor. Both vehicles belonged to Bob's father; the tractor, with its steel wheels, was purchased new for use on the farm. Bob and Andrew enjoy farming in the summer months and working on cars and tractors during the winter ★

The Groh family is proud their barn was chosen to help Ohio celebrate the Bicentennial. They continue to be amazed at both the number of visitors who stop and the distance some have traveled to view and photograph the barn. The family has enjoyed the experience of meeting new people and looks forward to making many new friends in 2003 ★

Butler

OWNER

Tari and Scott Spurlock

LOCATION

NW Corner of State Routes 73 and 177, in Oxford

On a warm summer day, travelers crossing through Davis Corners would not have been surprised to see Nell Davis sitting on the porch of her parents' Victorian home. With paper in hand, she took note of who was passing on the road in front of the Davis property, waving at those she knew. Nell, one of two daughters of Joseph and Laura Davis, was the social reporter for the Darrtown News and Oxford Press. For most of the twentieth century, even a visit to grandmother's for Sunday dinner merited mention in the social column. Nell and her sister, Maria, were well known in the community, having lived there all their lives. They knew everyone, and everyone knew them ★

The house that was their homestead was built in 1816. Located on 200 acres, it was moved to its present location in 1892 to avoid frequent flooding. A summer kitchen was located close behind the house. A former neighbor recalled that Laura Davis was frequently seen working in her large gardens, tending the produce that would be canned for her family to eat throughout winter ★

The barn was built by Joseph Davis, as shelter for his cattle and horses. He also raised hogs and chickens and grew corn and wheat. To help him on the farm, he hired an eighteen-year-old boy, Raymond Kane, to be his hired hand. Each fall the farmers used to have threshing parties to help with the harvest. It took at least ten men to accomplish the task, and the farmers took turns helping each other. The women prepared huge meals to feed the workers and would ring the dinner bell when the food was ready. The bell was loud enough to be heard by the men in the fields and could be heard on neighboring farms ★

The sisters, Nell and Maria, never married. After their mother died, in 1930, they looked after their father and took over the household chores. Nell did the cleaning, and Maria did the cooking and baking. A family friend remembered that Maria made the best molasses cookies she ever tasted, then or now. Throughout the house they had bookcases and cabinets filled with books and their individual collections. Nell collected salt bottles; Maria collected goblets. When required to feed the workers, they set a beautiful table for them, giving them individual salts, water goblets, good china, and cloth napkins ★

After Joseph died, Raymond continued to live in the house and ran the farm for Nell and Maria. After dinner, with tobacco and spittoon close at hand, he would settle in the alcove at the front of the house to read the daily newspaper. He was known for being neat, clean, and well organized. This extended from his personal appearance to the way he kept the barn. It was immaculate: floor always swept, tools hanging on pegs. Each horse had a section for its tack and equipment ★

Maria passed away in 1973 and Nell in 1982. The farmland they had so carefully tended was divided into parcels and sold. In September of 1991, Tari and Scott Spurlock purchased close to fifteen acres of the former Davis farm, including the house and barn ★

The house was practically original in condition; the sisters had made few changes. The cherry woodwork had never been painted, pocket doors never removed, and the summer kitchen and outhouse were still standing. It was all structurally sound but clearly in need of restoration ★

Debris lay everywhere in the barn. The previous owners had overloaded the hayloft, which had collapsed to the floor below. Tari and Scott cleaned it out and made necessary repairs. Although they are not farmers, they treasure the barn for the shelter it gives the many creatures they have adopted. Among the animals calling the barn home are llamas and alpacas, whose wool Tari spins. Goats, geese, a pot-bellied pig, horses, peacocks, chickens, and rabbits also live on the farm ★

Once the barn was stabilized, they began renovating the house. But in May of 2000, when the work was almost complete, a fire started in the summer kitchen and quickly spread to the home. The Spurlocks had retired for the evening, but a passing motorist saw the flames and pulled into the driveway. He pounded furiously on his car's horn, awakening the household. They immediately called for help and raced down the main staircase to safety. Their pets, which follow Tari wherever she goes, amazingly trotted right after her. Five fire departments responded to the call and did their job. The house, although gutted, did not burn to the ground ★

The Spurlocks built a new home on the property and moved forward with their lives. Since their barn was chosen to represent the county, preserving the history connected with both barn and property has become more important to them. They have always intended to restore the burned-out house and are considering the idea of a bed and breakfast. Their guests could enjoy the charm of days gone by in full view of Butler County's Bicentennial Barn. The Spurlocks' friendly menagerie would be happy to welcome them ★

Carroll

OWNER
Bob George

LOCATION
252 Waynesburg Road, north of Carrollton

Carroll County was formed on Christmas Day in 1832, its four hundred square miles taken from five adjoining counties. Largely an agricultural community, it was named for Charles Carroll, the last surviving person to sign the Declaration of Independence ★

The city of Carrollton, originally known as Centerville or Centretown, was laid out in 1815. A few miles north of the city is an intersection once known as Wherry's Crossing, now the junction of Waynesburg Road and State Route 43. For many years, the Wherry farm and homestead stretched across all four corners of the crossroads. Today, the historic corner is marked by Bob George's hundred-year-old barn, chosen as Carroll County's Bicentennial Barn ★

The Wherry family owned several hundred acres of farmland, making it one of the largest farms in the area. It passed from their family to the Underhills and then to Burt Turner. In 1962, Richard and Betty George, Bob George's aunt and uncle, purchased 130 acres from Turner. Richard bought and sold cattle and owned a slaughterhouse. After his death in 1986, his nephew Bob George purchased the farm ★

Both the barn and house on the property are at least one hundred years old. Neither has been fundamentally changed. The lower level of the barn is paved with brick; the upper level floor is wood. At some point, a straw shed was added to the barn, and in the process, someone left a small handprint in the concrete between the two structures. The highly visible barn was once used to advertise Mail Pouch Tobacco ★

Bob raises cattle, both beef and dairy. A collector of farm antiques, he has a variety of tools and horse-drawn equipment, including a Weber wagon.

His fourteen Belgian horses often appear in local parades and horse pulls. In addition to raising hay, which he rakes with help from his Belgians, Bob grows and sells pine trees ★

The newest resident of the barn is a sad-eyed, Brahma steer, and Bob considers it his most unusual purchase. The animals were originally bred in India and are considered sacred there. The breed has large, droopy ears, an excess amount of skin around the throatlatch and dewlap, and there is a pronounced hump in their back. They are inquisitive and shy, like affection, and can become quite docile ★

Bob George grew up on a farm in the area. As a lifelong farmer, he understands the importance of barns to Ohio's agricultural communities. He offered his barn to the Bicentennial Commission and is proud it was chosen to represent Carroll County. He is committed to maintaining his historic barn and house, thereby continuing the tradition of a farm at Wherry's Crossing ★

Champaign

Owner
Martha Lippencott

Location
1716 US Route 36, east of Urbana

Champaign County was created in 1805 from Greene and Franklin counties. Urbana, the county seat, was designed and surveyed the same year. Many of the early buildings still exist, surrounding the city's historic public square. Leading away from downtown, Route 36 is lined with elegant homes, displaying an eclectic mixture of architectural styles. The barn chosen to represent Champaign County sits on a farm just east of the city limits, as city gives way to countryside ★

Owned by Martha Lippencott and her late husband, Ronald, the barn and house were built in the 1920s by the Kenagy family. For a time, Oren Stickley owned the farm but sold it around 1940. Charles and Hattie Outram were the next occupants of the farmhouse, followed by their son, John, who took over in 1954. John Outram operated a dairy on the property and raised sheep ★

The Lippencotts purchased the 139-acre farm in 1963. Childhood sweethearts, Martha and Ronald were married just before World War II and were happy to finally have a farm of their own. They were partners; both had jobs in town and at night returned home to do chores. Martha remembers there were many times she milked their forty-five head of cattle by herself, while Ronald dealt with heavier tasks. The dairy barn was equipped with a milking parlor and cow stanchions, but those features were removed when the Lippencotts began raising beef cattle. They lost several of the animals when the east haymow collapsed in the 1970s. It has since been rebuilt ★

The Lippencotts' three children grew up on the farm and spent hours playing in the barn. Martha recalls her youngest son digging tunnels through bales of hay and straw. Accompanied by a neighborhood friend, the two boys could spend an entire afternoon crawling through their creation, followed by a faithful collie. Martha and Ronald were avid basketball players, a sport they both played at school. The barn still supports the basketball hoop Ronald put up for family games ★

The Lippencotts lived on the farm for only ten years before moving to another property. Their son continued to live on the property for several years. During that time, the interior of the farmhouse was extensively remodeled. His stepson lives there now and helps manage the farm. The barn is still home to cattle, but the number has been greatly reduced ★

Martha and Ronald were happy their barn was chosen to help the county celebrate Ohio's birthday. They quickly arranged to give it a new coat of paint before Scott Hagan arrived to paint the logo. Ronald lived long enough to see his barn become the Champaign County Bicentennial Barn, but he passed away a few months later. The couple had been together sixty-one years, and Martha misses him very much. When she looks at the barn, she thinks back to their first years on the farm. About how little they had when they first bought it, and how hard they worked to make it a success. It is the spirit shared by Ohio's first farmers, who strived to make a success of their farms in the wilderness 200 years ago ★

Clark

OWNER
Young's Jersey Dairy

LOCATION
6880 State Route 68, in Yellow Springs

The Clark County barn has the distinction of being the newest of the Bicentennial Barns. It has never been used to store hay or shelter livestock, is always warm and dry, and has a modern heating and cooling system. Located on the grounds of Young's Jersey Dairy, it can be found next to an eighteen-hole miniature golf course, whimsically labeled Udders and Putters. Built in 1997, the barn houses The Golden Jersey Inn restaurant ★

Relatives of the Young family have owned the land for over a hundred years. They built the original barn, which is still on the property, in 1869. Sometime after World War II, Hap Young purchased the sixty-acre farm, where he grew grain and raised hogs and cattle. When Hap and his three sons, Carl, Bob, and Bill, started to sell milk to the public, it was the beginning of a prosperous business. In 1960, they opened their first retail store, selling milk and other dairy products, including their homemade ice cream ★

The Youngs continued to expand the business. As their dairy store increased in popularity, they began serving food. Later they added a bakery and gift shop. In the 1990s, they decided to add a full service restaurant. They wanted it to look like a barn and reasoned that the best way to accomplish that was to build a barn ★

Known for their timber-frame homes, Riverbend Timber Framing of Blissfield, Michigan, was chosen to design and build the new structure. Following the same method that has been used for years, the oak frame was joined by mortise and tenon with wooden pins. The bents for the 6,600-

square-foot restaurant were assembled on the ground, and each weighed close to 8,000 pounds. In a bow to technology, the crew then used a crane to lift them into place ★

Young's Jersey Dairy has family oriented activities and events throughout the year. In keeping with the farm theme, the miniature golf course is dotted with a tiny barn and silo, a mill with waterwheel, numerous streams and fountains, and colorful lights. Near the old barn, at the opposite end of the complex, are a petting zoo and a barnyard full of friendly goats. Now, in addition to playing golf and eating ice cream, visitors can have dinner in Clark County's Bicentennial Barn. Oh yes, and you don't have to worry about bats ★

Clermont

OWNER
Lucy and Charles Snell

LOCATION
State Route 32, in Williamsburg

On September 11, 2001, barn painter Scott Hagan left the Snell house early in the morning. The Clermont County barn was to be dedicated that evening, and he wanted to make sure the painting would be complete in plenty of time. Lucy Snell knew something was wrong when he came racing back to the house. Scott had started painting, listening to the radio with his headphones on, when he heard the emergency broadcast about New York City. Together they sat down and, with the rest of the world, watched the tragedy unfold on television. Scott returned to the barn and finished painting the logo. That evening the barn was dedicated but with an understandably smaller crowd than anticipated ★

Lucy Snell had not really wanted her barn painted. She first read about the Bicentennial Barn project in a publication from the local electric company. Friends thought her barn was the perfect choice because it was so visible and well maintained. Eventually they convinced her to submit her name, and a local conservator from the Clermont County Historical Society presented her with an application. Forty barns were considered, but the Bicentennial representatives agreed with her friends, and the Snell barn was chosen. As with everything Lucy does, she entered into the spirit of the Bicentennial with enthusiasm. She began looking through her paperwork to see what she might have about the history of the barn. Even Lucy was amazed at the documents that had been saved by the original owner, T. J. Myers ★

Myers hired Elton Hauch and J. C. Manley to build the barn in 1939. Built as a tobacco barn, the construction was completed at a cost of $1,558.87. Lumber was ordered from Williamsburg Supply, and other material came from J. C. Fuhr Hardware in Williamsburg. The squat little barn measures sixty by forty feet, is twenty-five feet high, and can accommodate three and a half acres of drying tobacco ★

Lucy Snell inherited the barn in 1991 from T. J. Myers' son, Ecton. The Snells continue to raise tobacco, hay, corn, and soybeans, just as the Myers family did. They have made no changes to the barn; even the roof is original. Ecton Myers knew what he was doing when he left his farm to Lucy. He was proud of his heritage and his property. He worked hard to maintain the barn and very much wanted someone to care for it as he had. He found that person in Lucy Snell. The barn will stand for many years to come as a tribute to both the Myers family and Clermont County's agricultural history ★

Clinton

OWNER
Stewart and Lynn Alexander

LOCATION
901 New Oglesbee Road, in Wilmington

The barn chosen to represent Clinton County sits on a 300-acre farm a few miles north of Wilmington, the county's largest city. In 1976, Rendel Carey purchased the farm previously owned by Edwin Kirk. There were numerous barns and outbuildings on the property, including four houses, two of which were occupied by caretakers. Carey hired Stewart and Lynn Alexander to manage the farm, and in 1978, the couple moved into one of the houses on the farm ★

The old, white farmhouse was built in 1860, and it soon became home to the family. There, the Alexanders raised their two children, surrounded by acres of grain, corn, and soybeans. The children grew up playing in the shadows of the old barn, located a few hundred feet from the house ★

Built about the same time as the house, the barn's massive beams are joined by mortise and tenon, held in place with wooden pins. As caretakers of the property, the couple repaired the barn when necessary but made few changes. The Alexanders never dreamed that the barn they maintained would be chosen to help Ohio celebrate its 200th birthday ★

In 1995, Rendel Carey died, and two years later the Alexanders purchased the property. For several more years, their son, Ryan, lived in the house. In 2002, Stewart and Lynn Alexander decided to sell both house and barn, along with ten to twelve acres of land. Hopefully, the next owners will embrace the idea of having a Bicentennial Barn and will maintain it as the Alexanders did, for yet another generation to enjoy ★

Columbiana

OWNER
Sally, Courtney, and Connor Stewart

LOCATION
5707 State Route 45, in Lisbon

In the mid-1800s, Columbiana County was recognized as the greatest wool-growing county in Ohio, producing over half a million pounds each year. The county was also considered one of the best fruit-producing areas of the state, with raspberries being one of its most prolific crops ★

In the fall of 1863, a notable historic event occurred within the borders of the county. After terrorizing the southern counties of Ohio during a west to east rampage, Confederate General John Morgan surrendered in Salineville. His dash across the state began in July of 1863, when he crossed the Ohio River into Indiana and moved through Ohio in an attempt to recross the river at Marietta. With less than 2,000 troops, referred to as Morgan's Raiders, he pillaged small towns along the way. Ohioans breathed a collective sigh of relief at his capture ★

Representing this agricultural and historic county is the hundred-year-old barn owned by Sally Stewart and her children, Courtney and Connor. The dairy barn was built by the Halverstadt brothers, known in the area for building white barns ★

Stewart bought the seventy-six-acre farm north of Lisbon in 1993. The previous owners, the Baronzzi family, had operated an antiques store in the barn. Although they made necessary modifications to the main floor, the horse stalls remain in the lower level of the structure. The house the Stewarts live in was built by the Sadler family; the original farmhouse was lost to a fire ★

Sally Stewart purchased the property, not with an interest in farming, but with a love of the land. She enjoys taking long walks on her farm and having a safe place for her children to play. The barn simply came with the property and is used for storage. Seven years later, she was surprised and pleased when her barn was selected to represent Columbiana County ★

The barn was dedicated early in 2000. In the fall of 2002, Pittsburgh television station KDKA heard about the Bicentennial Barn project and came to Columbiana County to do a segment about the Stewarts and their barn. Scott Hagan returned to Lisbon to repaint the barn, which had badly faded. Proudly displaying its refreshed logo, the historic, white barn is ready to help Ohio and Columbiana County celebrate Ohio's Bicentennial ★

Coshocton

OWNER
John and Mary Powell

LOCATION
54210 US Route 36, in Fresno

When the Powell family first saw this land, with its rolling hills, winding lanes, and picturesque valleys, perhaps they were reminded of their homeland. Thomas J. and Henrietta Powell immigrated to the United States from Wales in 1817. They first lived in Virginia, moved north to Mingo Bottom, near Steubenville, and then finally settled in Coshocton County ★

Thomas and Henrietta rented a farm, while Thomas searched for ideal property to buy. In 1832, he purchased 1,080 acres from the heirs of Resin Davis. The land had been bestowed upon Davis by the United States government in gratitude for his service during the Revolutionary War. Thomas gave 400 acres to his oldest son, as compensation for selling the estate he left behind in Wales. Tradition dictates the oldest son inherits the land, but Thomas had to sell in order to purchase the new farm in Ohio ★

The Powells built a stone house on their property, where they raised their twelve children. Thirty years later, they watched as war tore apart their adopted country. As many Ohio families did, the Powells put themselves at risk by becoming involved with the Underground Railroad. In time, the farm was divided among their children. Seven generations later, their descendants are still calling this land home. A drive down County Road 93 takes visitors past the small Powell cemetery and farms owned by the family ★

In 1975, John Powell purchased a ninety-eight acre farm. Just around the corner from where he lived, the farm included a house and barn. Since 1927, it was owned by the Russell Little family. The farmhouse, a bungalow with wide front porch, was built between 1917 and 1918. In the process of updating the house, the Powells scraped off layers of wallpaper. They found the name and date, George Hill 1918, on one of the walls, but aren't sure of his connection to the house ★

The barn measures thirty-six feet, the standard width of a dairy barn, by sixty-four feet and has a side-wall pent roof. A pent roof resembles a forebay or overhang and provides protection for the stall areas. According to the date carved in one of the overhead beams, the barn was probably built in 1924 ★

The Powells' son, Brian, lives on the farm with his family. They grow corn and alfalfa, keep a herd of Holstein steers, and raise chocolate Labrador Retrievers ★

Painted in 1999, the Powells' barn was the first to have the logo on the linear side. The barn-painting project hadn't yet taken hold in Ohioans' hearts when the Powell barn was painted, and only a small group gathered for the dedication. As the popularity of the barns has increased, so has the number of visitors. The Powell family is proud of their heritage and is pleased to represent their county. Their tradition of farming will be handed to the next generation and with it: the Coschocton County Bicentennial Barn ★

Crawford

OWNER
Mike and Tammy Grady

LOCATION
3536 State Route 598, in Crestline

In 1840, when William C. Fisher built his barn, Crawford County was only twenty years old. The wood used in its construction came from timber felled in the woods on his property. At that time, Crawford County was still wilderness, but railroads soon arrived bringing progress and population growth. Not far from William's farm, the little town of Crestline was created at the junction of two rail lines. Originally called Livingston, it was laid out in 1851 ★

William's farm prospered and he soon built a large farmhouse on his property. Big enough for two families, his son, John, lived there after his marriage, helping his father look after the eighty-acre farm. John Fisher inherited the property after his father's death. He hired a carpenter to make new cabinets for the kitchen and remodeled the house from top to bottom ★

John also made changes to the barn. He doubled his storage space by dismantling a barn from a neighboring farm and reassembling it as an addition to his old barn. An overhang was added, to the side of the barn that faces the street, to protect some of his equipment from the weather. John's daughter, Ruth Schelk, has fond memories of growing up on the farm. A large herd of dairy cattle was kept in the lower level of the barn, and Ruth remembers there were always cats, cats, and more cats. Her uncle, who lived in Cleveland, came frequently to visit and always brought along Ruth's cousin. Together, the children played in the barn and on the ramp leading to the big double doors ★

John Fisher separated some of his property and sold it off in small lots. In 1975, the Fishers sold their remaining acres and moved to a house in town. Within five years, the big Victorian farmhouse burned to the ground. John Fisher had passed away by then, and Ruth Schelk is glad he didn't have to witness it. Her mother, she said, could handle anything and didn't seem fazed by the loss, but Ruth is still saddened when she thinks about it ★

One of John Fisher's lots was purchased by the Grady family. Their son, Mike, spent hours at the farm as he was growing up. He played hide and seek in the barn and enjoyed sliding down the barn's ramp, just as Ruth and her cousin had years before. Parties were held in the barn, and frequently there were barn dances on Saturday night ★

Mike Grady grew up with many fond memories of the farm, and when the property was again for sale, in 1997, he and his wife, Tammy, bought it. Now their children play in the barn and slide down the ramp. He has made few changes to the barn but has studied the inside closely. He can show you where the two barns are joined and point out the differences in their construction. The barn does have new doors; the Gradys lost the old ones the first year they lived there, when a powerful storm ripped them off ★

The Gradys are pleased their barn was selected to represent the county. So is Ruth Schelk, who thinks her father would have been very proud. So much of the original farm is gone, but Mike remembers what was there and appreciates the history the barn represents. He hopes to maintain it as a symbol of what came before and delights at seeing children play in it, as so many past generations have done ★

Fisher barn circa 1975.
Courtesy of Ruth Fisher Schelk.

OWNER
Norman Wengatz

LOCATION
7450 W 130 St, in Middleburg Heights

In 1840, Middleburg was a tiny community of a few hundred people. One hundred years later, Norman and Virgina Wengatz purchased property on Settlement Road. Although the population had increased by then, Settlement Road was still just a dirt lane. They named their farm Settledown, a combination of the road name and the fact that they had been looking for a place to settle down ever since Norman returned from World War II ★

In the subsequent sixty years, Middleburg grew up to become Middleburg Heights, a densely populated suburb of Cleveland. Settlement Road became West 130th Street and was widened to four lanes. Settledown Farm is surrounded by post-war housing, with neatly trimmed yards and paved sidewalks. In the midst of it all, defying progress to come any closer, the Wengatz's yellow barn stands tall as the Cuyahoga County Bicentennial Barn ★

In 1847, George and Anna Maria Haag emigrated from Reichenbach, Germany. Although it was a difficult journey, they did not face the uncertainty that some families faced. Earlier, a friend had agreed to find property for them when he came to America. When the friend located a place fitting George's specifications, he contacted them ★

The property he had in mind was owned by the Gardner family. It had seventy-four acres of land, two log houses, and a creek with a gristmill. George Haag came to an agreement with Gardner for the sale of the property, and the family moved into one of the log houses. In 1853, they built two barns and a brick house, which is still standing ★

George and Anna Maria divided their farm among their children. Leonard Haag owned twenty-five acres of the property, including one of the barns. Norman Wengatz, who grew up in nearby Parma, thought it was a wonderful farm. He had his eye on the property for a long time and finally approached Leonard about buying it. Haag didn't want to sell, but promised to call Norman if, and when, he decided to ★

Norman Wengatz returned from the war and married Virginia, his girl back home. Housing was difficult to find at that time, so the couple lived with his parents while searching for a place of their own. True to his word, Leonard Haag called Norman and said he was ready to sell his land. Norman remembers the offer was made on Sunday, and Leonard had a down payment on Monday. It was a bittersweet moment. Norman and Virginia were thrilled; Leonard Haag cried ★

In 1946, there was nothing else on Settlement Road. No houses, no electricity, and very few trees. Norman and Virginia paid to have electricity run to the farm and started building their house. Norman fenced in the farm and began a lifetime of raising registered Angus cattle ★

In 1966, Norman and Virginia sold most of their farm to a developer, retaining two and a half acres, including house and barn. Norman thinks his barn was built in 1915, but speculates it may have been moved from another site. It is now used only for storage ★

Norman and Virginia welcomed the notion of a Bicentennial Barn. The barn and the farm played a major role in their lives, and they were proud to share its history with the community. Unfortunately, Virgina passed away less than a year after the barn was painted. She was looking forward to welcoming visitors to Settledown Farm throughout the Bicentennial celebrations. She is missed by her friends and family, and for Norman, nothing is quite the same without her ★

Darke

OWNER
Fred and Pat McMaken

LOCATION
5361 Requarth Road, in Greenville

Formed in 1809, Darke County was named for General William Darke. A farmer from his youth, he served in the Revolutionary War, was taken prisoner during the battle of Germantown, Pennsylvania, and later sat on the Virginia Legislature. The county seat is Greenville, built on the site of a fort, where the Treaty of Greenville was signed in 1795. Hopeful that hostilities between Indian tribes and settlers were going to cease, many farmers sought to buy property in the area. The McMaken Bicentennial Barn sits on property settled in the early years of Darke County ★

The first owner of the property appears to be William Wilson. He sold acreage to Thomas Briggs in 1828. In 1871, Christian Miller assumed the mortgage to the 108-acre farm. Christian's son, Lewis, built the existing house in 1872 to replace one lost to fire. It is likely he also built the barn to shelter his horses and cattle. The property stayed in the Miller family until December 1991 ★

When Fred and Pat McMaken purchased the farm in 1991, there remained only five acres of the original farm, including the house and barn. The house was remodeled and doubled in size in 1936, but no significant changes were made after that. As the McMakens worked on the house, they finally inspected the attic and discovered it had not been cleaned out. Fred and Pat found many family treasures and boxes of photographs and negatives ★

The McMakens tracked down the family and gave them the personal items. Fred and Pat were pleased to be able to keep some of the old images of the house and farm. Looking at the faded pictures gives them a sense of the history they are now a part of and an added incentive to preserve it ★

Together, the McMakens have slowly renovated the old farmhouse. Work on the barn has been slow, as it needs extensive repairs. The mortar holding the old fieldstones together has crumbled, and the siding is rotting. When they saw an advertisement in the local paper about the barn-painting project, they knew they had a great location but were dubious about being chosen. They submitted an application anyway ★

Selected to represent Darke County, the McMaken barn represents the early farming traditions of the county. They are proud to be caretakers of the property and will try to preserve the barn for as long as possible. The family welcomes you to the Darke County Bicentennial Barn ★

Defiance

OWNER

Mark and Louise Schreiber

LOCATION

18622 State Route 15, in Defiance

Money may not buy happiness, but it most certainly can buy a Bicentennial Barn. Mark and Louise Schreiber were looking for property in the country, when their realtor suggested a farm south of Defiance. They loved the old farmhouse at once, but were surprised they hadn't been told about the huge barn, painted with a very distinctive logo. Although they weren't quite sure what they were getting into, they bought it anyway ★

The Schreiber family purchased the property from Mike and Kathy Boff in 2000. Not long after, they were sent a history of the farm prepared by Esther Grant, daughter of the original owners. The family learned that many years ago there was a log cabin on the property, near where the barn is located. The existing farmhouse was the homestead of Jesse and Ada Grant and was built in 1900. A small building, still standing near the house, was originally a blacksmith shop ★

Jesse Grant was a cattleman and in 1926 built the barn we know as the Defiance County Bicentennial Barn. Two years later, he purchased an older barn and had it moved to his property. The two barns were connected to form one L-shaped structure ★

The barn is immense. Square footage totals 6,400 feet, with the longest side measuring 115 feet. Stables, stalls, and pens are still in place, and the long feed alley is a source of great amusement to the Schreibers' numerous, surefooted cats. Standing in the upper level, the mow soars thirty-two feet to the rafters, providing an attractive home for the neighborhood colony of bats. The barn is in amazingly good condition, and with a small amount of work, it could accommodate a large quantity of livestock ★

The Schreibers are not quite sure what they are going to do with the barn. Louise home-schools their three children: Lydia, Carolyn, and Camden. They are looking at ventures that would involve the whole family in some aspect of the business. Lydia has joined 4-H; she and Carolyn are animal lovers. Their horses occupy stalls in the barn, and they look after the cats and kittens. The girls are particularly fond of a little Jersey Wooly rabbit they have named Cadbury ★

Many relatives of the Grant family remain in the area and feel a strong attachment to the land of their ancestors. Knowing the background has given them a greater appreciation of the farm and is an ongoing history lesson for their children. As custodians of the barn, Mark and Louise feel a responsibility to maintain it for the community. They are quick to point out that while two gables are painted with the logo, the State of Ohio only sponsored one. The other logo was commissioned and paid for by the Defiance County Historical Society. The Schreiber family is proud to own the Defiance County Bicentennial Barn and is happy to welcome visitors to their farm ★

Delaware

OWNER
Sue Postle and Irena Scott

LOCATION
6844 Bale Kenyon Road, in Lewis Center

The barn chosen to represent Delaware County greets travelers approaching Columbus on southbound Interstate 71. Located on a farm just north of the Polaris Parkway interchange, the property has been continuously occupied since 1812 by descendants of Lee Hurlburt. Built in a day when horses were harnessed to plow the fields, the barn was once surrounded by acres of peacefully grazing sheep and neighboring farms ★

Lee Hurlburt was one of the first settlers in Delaware County. He bought property on the east side of Alum Creek, where he built a log cabin for his family. A frame house, still standing, was built on the site in 1825. Sisters, Sue McCammon Postle and Irena McCammon Scott, Hurlburt's great-great-granddaughters, now own the farm. Sue and her husband, Bob, live in the farmhouse, designated a Historic Ohio Homestead in 1977 ★

Over the years, Lee Hurlburt's acreage was divided into three separate but adjoining farms. His granddaughter, Zelma, married John McCammon, and they had four children, one daughter and, conveniently, three sons. The boys eventually chose which farm they wanted to live on ★

Two of the farms had nice houses. Jim McCammon chose the one with the new barn, which included the old homestead and one hundred acres. The barn was built by Lee Hurlburt's son, Ezra, in 1900. He hired Burt Hamilton, of Westerville, to do the framing, and the family put on the siding. The timber frame is made of beech, the siding of poplar, the roof of slate ★

Jim and his wife, Gay, raised their family in the farmhouse, as previous generations had done. Their three children: John, Irena, and Sue were taught at an early age to drive a team of horses and help on the farm. The McCammons operated a sheep farm, and Jim always had several hundred grazing in his fields. Jim loved his sheep, and Irena recalls the racket they made whenever he approached the barn. They took little notice of the rest of the family; after all, they knew who fed them. Jim sold the wool from his flock until the price plummeted. Eventually, he leased fifty of his acres to a nursery and used the other fifty for hay ★

Jim McCammon's barn and beloved sheep. Courtesy of Irena Scott.

A farmer all his life, he was used to heights. Sue and Irena recall the occasion a family with small children came to the farm for a visit. Children are always drawn to a barn, and these were no exception. In a short time, one of them had climbed to the top of the barn and made his way along one of the purlin timbers, running lengthwise across the barn. Predictably, he lost his nerve and refused to move forward or backward. Much to everyone's amazement, Jim McCammon calmly and deliberately walked down the beam and rescued his terrified guest ★

Jim McCammon died in 1995. Sue and Bob Postle moved into the farmhouse in 1998. Bob has become as attached to the barn as his father-in-law was and has devoted much of his spare time to working on it. The barn has new slate on the roof, the siding has been replaced, and any weaknesses reinforced. Bob recently purchased a forty-six-foot, twenty-ton lift truck, intent upon repairing the cupola ★

76

The landscape around the homestead has changed dramatically since the 1950s. Alum Creek was dammed, which flooded out several farms that had existed for years. Highways have come through, followed by other signs of progress: housing developments, fast-food restaurants, and mega-sized shopping malls. Although some of Lee Hurlburt's original farm has been divided and sold, most of it is still owned by Bales and McCammons. Sue, Irena, and Bob are proud of their heritage and are committed to preserving the family homestead. With Bob Postle as caretaker, the family barn will continue to stand, preserving the family's tradition of farming and evoking fond memories of a distant lifestyle ★

Erie

OWNER
Steinen Family

LOCATION
Perkins Avenue, in Huron

Six generations of Steinens have grown up on the 200-acre farm that surrounds Erie County's Bicentennial Barn. The present owner, Gil Steinen, has the original deed to the property, which is dated 1870. The old homestead, where so many family members were born and raised, still stands on a lane secluded from the main road ★

There have been some changes. A railroad and a state route now bisect the property. For many years, there were three barns on the farm. In the early 1920s, the county road department was working in the area. Each night they parked their equipment in the Steinens' yard. One morning, when they started their steam engines, the sparks ignited some nearby straw stacks, causing a massive fire that destroyed all of the barns ★

Gil's grandfather, Dave Steinen, built the existing barn in 1925. It measures forty-seven feet tall, eighty feet long, and sixty feet wide. Livestock, including hogs, sheep, and cattle, were sheltered within its walls. Horses called the barn home then and now, but in earlier days they had to work for their oats. Horses were a necessity on a farm. There were no tractors, and the horses had to pull the plows that cultivated fields of crops ★

Gil fondly recounts a story about his grandfather's first tractor. The elderly man had grown up cultivating with horses, but in the early 1940s, he decided to purchase a small tractor. Now, on their property there was a creek with a fence to keep the cattle on the bank. As he approached the creek, he hollered "whoa," but the tractor, not yet used to verbal commands, proceeded forward and ended up overturned in the water ★

When Gil came home from school that afternoon, he found his grandfather devastated because he thought he had killed his new tractor. Fortunately, Gil's schooling included a course in auto mechanics. In a couple of hours, after draining the oil and gas, Gil had it dried out and up and running. He still has the tractor, a Farmall A, and is planning to restore it as a gift for his granddaughter who graduated from college in the fall of 2002 ★

The Steinen barn represents a long tradition of farming, but that will soon be coming to an end. Gil and his family are in the process of donating their land to the local park system. As a tribute to the ancestor who began it all, Gil's great-grandfather, the proposed name for the new park is the Joe Steinen Wildlife Area. In a time when many of the family farms are being sold to developers, this one will remain much as it was when the first Steinen set foot upon it ★

Fairfield

OWNER
John and Donna Brown

LOCATION
4367 State Route 158, in Lancaster

Even before the Spirit of St Louis made its historic transatlantic flight, aviator Charles Lindbergh was thrilling spectators at air shows across the country. His hectic schedule was called barnstorming and included frequent stops at small airstrips. On a visit to Ohio, Lindbergh landed at an airfield in the middle of Sam Campbell's farm, which lies on the outskirts of Lancaster. As he entertained his audience, Lindbergh soared over cornfields and pastures. He also flew over Campbell's dairy barn, a barn that is still standing today as Fairfield County's Bicentennial Barn ★

The 146-acre farm was purchased by T. S. Bright around 1883. Bright first built a small summerhouse to live in and then began constructing the barn in 1884. The barn is built of mortise and tenon construction, and huge logs were used in the framing. It measures ninety-six feet in length, is sixty-five feet wide, and stands fifty feet high. One year later, he built a farmhouse for his family, carving his name into stone in the basement ★

By 1934, Porter K. Brown had set his sights on acquiring the farm. It took him two years, but owner Sam Campbell finally agreed to sell. The airfield was no longer is use, but the hangar contained two planes, which were soon removed. Although Porter's son, John, had big ideas about learning to fly, Porter dismantled the hangar and rebuilt it closer to the barn where it would be more useful. Other changes included the removal of the milking parlor. A two-story structure, it had an elevator to take grain to the second floor ★

John Brown grew up in the farmhouse facing Lancaster–Kirkersville Road, now State Route 158. It was a brick road, as he recalls, all the way north to Baltimore. His father raised cattle and hogs, and grew corn and grain. An only child, John helped his father load straw and hay into the mow of the barn. Although farming was hard work, there was always time to have fun, and John has memories of riding the hay hook up to the top ★

Eventually, the summerhouse was moved a few feet away from the main house, but retained the original wood siding, large fireplace, and chimney. The house John was raised in received numerous updates, most notably to the kitchen. Remodeled and enlarged in the late 1940s, it was outfitted in the popular style of the day with white metal cabinets made by Youngstown Kitchen. John and Donna Brown built their own home on the property, not far from his parents' farmhouse, in 1966 ★

The barn, consistently maintained over the years, is home to the Brown's herd of purebred Polled Herefords. John and Donna proudly stood by as it was painted and dedicated. They are sure John's parents would be pleased to know their barn was chosen to be part of Ohio's birthday celebration. John and Donna Brown are looking forward to the Bicentennial events in 2003 and welcome visitors to the farm ★

Fayette

OWNER
Colin and Julie Campbell

LOCATION
8473 State Route 41, north of Washington Court House

Long before their children married, the Dills and the Campbells had something in common. Both families had lived in Ross County in the town of Bainbridge, where Colin Campbell owned a general store. The Dills were the first to move away, and they settled in Dill Station, a little village that was a railroad stop. Both families then moved to Fayette County in the 1880s ★

Hays and Lettitia Dill bought a large farm north of Washington Court House. In 1914, Hays decided that the existing barn no longer suited his needs, and he proudly ordered a new one from the Sears and Roebuck catalog. The materials for the barn had not yet been delivered when he unexpectedly passed away ★

Determined to go forward with the project, Lettitia saw it through to completion. The brick foundation was constructed and the framing put together and raised. A distinctive stamped metal roof was preassembled and delivered to the farm in sections. The decorative cupolas, designed to provide ventilation for the loose hay stored in the mow, were set in place ★

Lettitia and Hays had four children, but only Dorothy and Frank lived to adulthood. Dorothy married Colin Campbell in the 1920s. Frank continued to live in the Dill farmhouse with his wife and five children. The Dill children belonged to 4-H clubs and raised sheep, hogs, rabbits, and chickens. The family had a large herd of milk cows, and the Dill boys had to milk them each morning before school ★

Howard and Frank Dill have wonderful memories of growing up on the farm. They loved playing in the barn but didn't want to be responsible for their younger brother. Brother David was just learning to walk and tried to follow his brothers everywhere. Frank recalls the day the older boys headed for the barn, and David tried his best to keep up with them. Inspiration hit. The brothers slowed him down by loading his diaper with apples from the orchard ★

Howard was the oldest and had his first driving accident when he was only six. There was no age or license requirement, and as long as he stood up, he could peer over the hood. One afternoon, he and his brothers took the family car, a Model T, and went to the store for their mother. Although warned not to, they bought candy with the money left over from their purchase. The boys were so excited that Howard started paying more attention to the candy than his driving and drove off the road ★

The car was not seriously damaged. They soon had it back on the road, drove home, and hid it in the garage. Much to his brothers' dismay, little David had smashed his nose, and it continued to bleed. Thinking quickly, they dunked his head in the horses' water trough to stop the flow. They might have gotten away with the accident, except that David started crying at dinner, and the truth came out. Howard still laughs when he tells the story. He insists that his mother's happiest day was when she was able to put all five of her children on a school bus at the same time ★

Dorothy Dill Campbell's son, Colin, now owns the farm. Campbell and his family live in the restored farmhouse and use the barn only for storage. They have no livestock but continue to farm the land, growing corn and soybeans. Colin Campbell is proud of his barn and committed to preserving it for years to come. When the barn was dedicated, members of both the Dill and Campbell families attended. Howard and Frank Dill are pleased that the Campbells have taken such good care of the farm that holds so many happy memories for them. The barn's striking silver cupolas will continue to sparkle in the sunlight, welcoming all who come to visit ★

Franklin

OWNER
The New Albany Company

LOCATION
*7519 Dublin–Granville Road,
in New Albany*

Franklin County, named for statesman Benjamin Franklin, was formed in 1803. Within its borders lies Columbus, a city carved from the wilderness to be Ohio's designated state capital. When the first census was taken in 1815, the population was listed as a mere 700. By the year 2000, it had increased to over 700,000. As the population grew, the city expanded through annexation, and farmland gave way to suburban sprawl ★

The barn chosen to represent Franklin County can be found in the small, affluent community of New Albany, just east of the Columbus city limits. Located in historic Plain Township, the area was once part of the United States Military District. The District was created in 1796, as the government set aside 2.5 million acres for Revolutionary War veterans. Soldiers were entitled to one-hundred-acre lots, but wealthy entrepreneurs often bought the rights from soldiers who did not want the land or could not afford to keep it. In that way, large farms were put together, and subsequently sold or inherited by the entrepreneurs' families ★

Dennis B. Strait came to Plain Township from New Jersey in 1839. Dennis became the area's most notable farmer, assembling close to 1,100 acres of land. He was known for his success in raising large herds of cattle and sheep. The house he built in 1851 is still standing. Bricks for its construction came from clay on the property and were fired in a kiln set up nearby. Walnut trees were cut for use as interior woodwork, including the doors, moldings, and staircase ★

After his death, the property went to his wife, Ann. It was later sold to Cap Williamson, who is credited with building the barn. In 1922, Cap sold the farm to Whitney Strait, Dennis Strait's son. The 500 acres stretched across all four corners of the intersection of Granville and Kitzmiller Roads. Whitney did not want to farm it, so he leased the land to W. Jonathan Garner, called Sled by his friends, and his wife, Josie Gartner Garner ★

In 1924, the Garners and their three daughters moved into the brick farmhouse. Sled Garner farmed the land and raised Jersey, Guernsey, and Holstein cattle. Eventually, Whitney Strait sold his farm, and the Garners purchased a portion of it. They worked hard to make a success of their venture, and everyone in the family helped ★

Dorothy Garner Appleton has many memories of life on the farm. She recalls the time her father dug a large hole in the ground to create a space for the hogs to feed. He filled the indention with bread, added corn and other grain, and covered it for the night with a washtub. Moisture from the earth, coupled with perhaps a bit of overnight rain, combined to expand the bread. In the morning, the family looked out the window to see the washtub perched on top of the bread, now swollen like a giant soufflé ★

In the mid-1950s, Sled and Josie built a house across the street. After spending a short time in the new house, they decided they liked the old one better and moved back. In 1959, Dorothy and her husband, Louis, bought the new house from her parents, and she has lived there ever since. From her window, she can look across the street and see the old brick house and, behind it, the barn and silo ★

The New Albany Company purchased the farm after Josie Garner's death. Dorothy Appleton is pleased to have them as caretakers of the farm and feels they have done a wonderful job of restoring the barn. She wishes her parents and husband could have lived to attend the dedication of the Bicentennial Barn. Dorothy is grateful it will remain standing to remind another generation of what life was once like in Franklin County ★

Fulton

OWNER
Lowell and Pat Rupp

LOCATION
21157 US Route 20A, in Archbold

Lowell Rupp is understandably proud of his farm. The land was owned by his family even before Fulton County was created. Formed in 1850, the county was once part of Lucas, Henry, and Williams counties. Settlements grew slowly on heavily forested land once known as the Black Swamp. As these communities expanded, residents decided to petition the State of Ohio for a county of their own. They named it Fulton after Robert Fulton, the inventor of the steamboat, and established the county seat at Wauseon ★

The Fulton County Bicentennial Barn, owned by Lowell and Pat Rupp, is located near the city of Archbold. Once a small farming community, it was first settled by families of French descent. On October 7, 1835, Christian and Magdalina Rupp purchased land from the United States government. The original deed bears the seal of President Andrew Jackson ★

The Rupps' eighty-acre farm was situated in an area known as Lauber Hill, named for one of the first families to settle there. The farm remained in the Rupp family, and in 1914, Lowell's grandparents, Henry and Cora Lauber Gearig, bought the farm. When Cora passed away in 1967, Lowell purchased the farm the following year ★

The barn was built by John and Elizabeth Sower. The Rupps assume it was constructed in 1881, based on the date carved into the old wooden door to the granary. The bank barn was completely re-sided in the late 1950s by

Lowell's grandparents, who did general farming. They kept their livestock in the barn and stored hay and grain ★

Lowell's mother grew up in the farmhouse next to the barn. Somewhat reluctantly, he sold it a few years ago along with a small parcel of land. The current owners love living in an old house next to the historic barn, since they have no farming responsibilities of their own. They have totally restored the home in a historically accurate fashion, and Lowell is pleased they are taking such good care of it ★

Growing up, Lowell accompanied his parents on visits to the farm and always looked forward to playing in the barn. As a child, he never gave a thought to one day being the caretaker of family memories. Today, the barn is no longer home to livestock and is only used for storage of machinery and equipment, but Lowell carefully maintains it ★

The Rupps saw an article in the Toledo Blade newspaper, asking for nominations for a barn in Fulton County, but regional coordinator, Beth Hansen, spotted the barn before they could fill out the necessary paperwork. Lowell and Pat Rupp are proud to own the Fulton County Bicentennial Barn and feel it is a fitting tribute to the Rupps and other families that settled on Lauber Hill so many years ago ★

Gallia

OWNER
Bob Evans Farms

LOCATION
State Route 588, in Rio Grande

Autumn in Ohio brings crisp morning air and a landscape of ever changing colors. Weekends find residents and tourists, young and old, heading for long country drives and partaking of the great American pastime of going out for breakfast. For Ohio's farmers, autumn brings the harvest: working in the fields for as long as there is daylight, praying for one more day without rain. In Gallia County, visitors can appreciate both worlds at the annual Bob Evans Farm Festival ★

Held in October, the event honors the tradition of the harvest by combining farming demonstrations with history, crafts, and country music. Food, that very important part of any festival, can be enjoyed in the barn, temporarily converted to a dining hall. While diners enjoy their repast, they can also admire the heavy timber framework around them. Not just any barn, this historic structure is Gallia County's Bicentennial Barn ★

The history of Bob Evans Farms begins in 1953 with the purchase of property by Bob and Jewell Evans. The farm, near Rio Grande, included a brick, Federal-style farmhouse owned by one of the area's first settlers, Nehemiah Wood. Built in 1820, the former coaching inn became home to Bob, Jewell, and their six children ★

There were several outbuildings on the farm, including two barns. One is a gambrel-roof barn built after 1900. The Bicentennial Barn was built around 1843 and designed to dry tobacco. Records indicate it was called the Brown barn, a reference relating to a previous owner, not the barn's color. The barn is considered a bank barn, with one side built into higher ground, resulting in two levels. One or more sheds have been added to the lower level, giving the barn its present sloping appearance ★

Bob and Jewell Evans lived on the farm for seventeen years. Bob Evan Farms purchased the property in 1970 and turned it into a tourist attraction. For outdoor lovers, they offer canoeing on nearby Raccoon Creek, camping, and horseback riding. For the less energetic, there are friendly critters to pet, a craft center to shop in, and a full-service Bob Evans Restaurant ★

Historians will be interested in the Revolutionary War cemetery and log cabin village. Called Adamsville Village, there are six restored cabins, transporting the visitor back to life in the early 1800s. Rio Grande was originally called Adamsville after its first settler, Adam Rickabaugh. A stone bearing his name can be found in the cemetery next to the village. Also interred are several members of the Wood family, including Harrison, Mary, and Bethsama. Not far from the Wood homestead, it may have once been a family cemetery. Most of the old stones are worn by nature and difficult to read; the earliest legible date is 1845 ★

The Wood farmhouse has been closed to the public since the Evans family left in 1970. Listed on the National Register of Historic Places, it was carefully restored in 2002 and will house the Homestead Museum. Scheduled to open in spring 2003, the museum will focus on the history of the farm, the company, and the Evans family ★

Bob Evans Farms is proud to have their barn represent Gallia County. They have strived to preserve the history of the property and be good neighbors to the community. Whether you stop to view the barn, eat in the restaurant, or attend one of the special events held throughout the year, they are pleased to welcome you to the farm ★

Geauga

OWNER

Jim and Pam Cermak

LOCATION

13034 Madison Road, north of Middlefield

Geauga County, founded in 1805, was the second county created in Connecticut's Western Reserve. Located in the heart of northeast Ohio's snowbelt, it experiences record snowfalls, colorful fall foliage, and is known for maple syrup production. In the spring, maple lovers flock to the area to attend the annual Maple Festival. Appropriately, the barn chosen to represent the county sits on a sugar maple farm, the Cermaks' Sugarbush Creek Farm ★

The property was first acquired in 1799 by Robert Breck, who bought all of lot 25 in Huntsburg Township from the Connecticut Land Company. Gradually, he sold off parcels of land, dividing up the 15,360 acres he originally purchased. Solomon Paine purchased 154 of those acres in 1823, and it remained in his family until 1882. The following year, the Bartholomew family, George W. and Angeline and their son and daughter-in-law, G. Alba and Florence, purchased the land, operating a dairy farm there until the 1930s ★

In 1992, Jim Cermak purchased the farm, by then reduced to fifty-nine acres. Harold McNish, the previous owner, had rented the farm to Amish families for many years. The property included a barn, outbuildings, and a house that was built in 1830 with no heat or electricity ★

Cermak spent long hours working on the house, installing wiring, and adding modern conveniences. Although the house has been altered by several additions, it still retains the charm of the era. Most of the interior woodwork is original, and the basement displays the huge tree trunks used as floor joists when the house was built ★

The former dairy barn measures 156 by 70 feet. Close examination reveals it is actually two bank barns joined together, end to end, with two ramps and separate entrances. One of the barns is over one hundred years old and was probably built when the Paine family lived there. The second barn may have been added by the Bartholomews, when more space was needed for their dairy operation. It is not known whether it was built on site or dismantled and moved to its present location ★

Some recent changes have been made to the barn, although not by design. When Cermak purchased the farm, the barn had a slate roof and two silos. A scant year later, a mini tornado ripped off the whole roof, wrapping much of it around a nearby tree. The vicious storm demolished one of the silos and then turned its wrath on the house, demonstrating its power by pulling an area rug straight up the staircase. Repairs were made as required, and the barn now sports a gleaming standing-seam roof, installed by members of Middlefield's Amish community ★

The Cermaks have worked hard to maintain the property and build their business. Jim has been involved in maple syrup production since he was twelve years old. Forty-five acres of his property are populated with over 2000 sugar maples. The trees are tapped in early spring, and the syrup is made in a sugarhouse tucked away in the woods. In 2000, they decided to enter their syrup in local fairs and festivals. Much to their delight, they received first place honors at the Geauga County Maple Festival, the Ohio State Fair, and the Great Geauga County Fair ★

Besides syrup and maple candy, the Cermaks sell equipment used in the industry, such as containers, tubing, condensers, and evaporators, that are imported from Canada. They host seminars and tours and hold classes in chain-saw education and wood-lot management. The small building the Cermaks use as a workshop was once a drive-through corncrib ★

The barn is now used primarily for storage of their equipment, but occasionally the Cermaks have found other uses for it. For several years in a row, they held gala Fourth of July barn parties, drawing over 200 people. The Cermaks now have three young sons, and having big parties isn't quite as easy as it used to be. However, Jim hopes to throw a party in 2003 that will rival his previous events. It will celebrate the Bicentennial and honor their barn, built on property once owned by an early settler in the wilderness of the Western Reserve ★

Greene

OWNER
Richard and Jean DeWine

LOCATION
3630 US Route 42, east of Cedarville

In 2003, as Ohio celebrates its Bicentennial, Greene County will be celebrating its own 200th birthday. One of Ohio's oldest counties, it was named for Nathaniel Greene, a Revolutionary War general. Early settlers erected sawmills near the many rivers and streams that flow through the county. Small farming communities developed near the mills, as families banded together. The barn chosen to represent Greene County can be found in just such a place. It is east of the small village of Cedarville and a few miles south of the historic mill town of Clifton ★

The hundred-year-old barn is owned by Richard and Jean DeWine. They purchased the surrounding farm from the Townsley family in 1967. Consisting of eighty-seven acres, the property included a house, two barns, and several outbuildings. The DeWines were well known in the area. For many years, Richard's father and uncle operated a prosperous seed company in Springfield ★

Richard used the farm to raise a herd of registered Black Angus cattle. Cows were brought into the barn to give birth, and Richard would hand-feed calves rejected by their mothers. In the mid-1970s, he rented the farmhouse to Roy Conover, the local postmaster. For the next 26 years, Roy and Judy Conover lived on the farm. Their three children grew up there and were involved in 4-H. They raised a variety of animals, and Richard generously allowed them to use the barn for their projects ★

To determine the age of the Bicentennial barn, the DeWines invited an expert to examine it. In his opinion, the barn dates to 1880. The former dairy barn has a sturdy timber frame of mortise and tenon construction. The upper-level floor is the original wood, while the lower level is concrete. The barn has been maintained as needed, including replacement of the siding ★

The rambling farmhouse was built about the same time as the barn, but has been expanded at least twice. It is easy to see where the additions were added; there are differences in the size and use of moldings and windows. The main staircase leads from the room once likely used as the parlor and has a graceful balustrade and newel cap ★

Recently, Roy and Judy Conover moved into a home of their own. It is new with modern conveniences and airtight windows, but Judy misses the old farmhouse. On a trip back to the farm, she reminisced about the days when her children were growing up. One of the Conovers' two sons met his future wife on the farm. An animal lover, she wanted to see the birth of a calf, and he invited her at the next opportunity. After that, she was a frequent visitor to watch the animal's progress ★

Roy and Judy are pleased their children were able to experience life on a farm. One of their sons loved the land enough to become a full-time farmer. He works for the grain farmer who leases land from the DeWines. The cattle are gone now, and the barn is strangely silent. It is used only for the storage of equipment ★

The barn dedication brought over 200 people to the farm. One of the guests was the previous owner of the farm, ninety-five-year-old Mr. Townsley. Although the barn is no longer used for livestock or dairy farming, it stands as a tribute to the hard work of the farmers who settled this area 200 years ago. The love of farming continues, instilled in Roy and Judy Conover's son, who seems determined to follow the tradition ★

Guernsey

OWNER
Robert and Kimberly Smith

LOCATION
250 Fair Avenue, in Fairview

In 1806, the city of Cambridge was designed and platted. Families from the British Isle of Guernsey were among the first to purchase lots. When the county was formed in 1810, they named it for their homeland. The barn chosen to represent Guernsey County is part of the small village of Fairview, near Quaker City. The barn can be seen, and easily photographed, from the entrance ramp of Route 40A onto westbound Interstate 70. A mere glimpse of the barn is not enough, however. Staying on to explore its surroundings is a wonderful opportunity to get to know the area which early settlers once called Pennyroyaldom ★

The name refers to a district composed of three townships bordering Belmont County and centered in Oxford Township. The first residents of the area found an abundance of the herb, Pennyroyal. A species of Mint, the leaves can be dried for tea or distilled to produce medicinal oil. In the early days of the county, farmers could harvest the herb for ready cash if weather or blight caused their crops to fail ★

When Highway 40, the National Road, was the main east-west road across the state, Fairview flourished. There were livery stables, several stores, pubs, houses, and a post office. The barn was built between 1908 and 1916, when W. G. and Rosa Cole owned the property. In 1921, Harry P. Sharkey operated a livery stable in the barn, later selling the property to Clint Bond. Bond's heirs sold the farm to Neal and Rosa Boyd in 1935 ★

The next owners of the barn were Emerson R. and Mary Arnold. Owners of the Home Telephone Company, they purchased the land on October 30, 1939. The barn became headquarters for the telephone workers, who met there to get their orders before going to the field. Equipment, supplies, and company vehicles were stored in the barn and on the property ★

Fairview became a sleepy little town, overwhelmed by Interstate 70, which was constructed just a hundred feet from the south side of the barn. In 1984, the Arnolds sold the property to Robert and Kimberly Smith, who use the barn for storage ★

The Smiths are pleased their barn was chosen to represent Guernsey County and are surprised at the traffic the barn-painting project has brought to the area. Bikers and auto clubs have scheduled outings and rallies for their members to visit the barn. There seems to be a renewed interest in Fairview. Houses in town are being restored, and the old grange hall has been reborn as the Pennyroyal Opera House. On the third Friday of each month, the town is treated to some of the top bluegrass bands in the country. The Guernsey County Bicentennial Barn stands ready to welcome visitors to the county and to Pennyroyaldom ★

Hamilton

OWNER
Bernie Fiedeldey

LOCATION
7941 E Miami River Road, in Colerain Township

In the early 1900s, the fertile land along the east
bank of the Great Miami River was a desirable place
to live. The winding lanes, which meandered
through Colerain Township, were lined with low
stone walls, and tidy farms dotted the landscape.
Historical society records indicate the area was
settled in 1790 by John Dunlap, a surveyor from
Coleraine, Ireland. Coleraine Township, as it was
spelled then, was created in 1794 ★

Those who bought property, kept it in the family by passing it on to their
heirs. As times changed, families grew smaller, and there was less interest
in farming. The population grew older, and it became more difficult for
owners to maintain their farms. Gradually, homes fell into disrepair, barns
collapsed, and the stone walls, that had given the area such distinction,
began to crumble ★

In 1995, Bernie and JoAnn Fiedeldey found a twenty-five acre parcel for
sale on East Miami River Road. Previously owned by the Bachmann family,
the property included a farmhouse and barn. Caroline and Estella
Bachmann grew up there and stayed on the farm after their father, George,
passed away. Neighbors remember the two maiden ladies sold hay and straw,
and kept chickens and two milk cows in their barn. Estella died in the mid-
1980s, and in the early 1990s, Caroline went into a nursing home, never
to return to the farmhouse ★

When the Fiedeldeys took possession of the property, it was like walking
into a time warp. The years had stood still for the sisters; they had changed
nothing, including their outhouse. The Fiedeldeys went to work on the

house, totally remodeling the inside, but they painstakingly restored the exterior to retain its original appearance ★

The barn was in complete disrepair and overgrown with weeds. It wasn't until they cleared away the brush that they were able to see the stone foundation and wall. The roof had leaked for years and caused considerable damage to the second floor, which had sunk three or four feet. Although it was a daunting task, Bernie decided to save the barn, anyway ★

He tore out approximately two-thirds of the second floor and rebuilt it. Every board in the barn was renailed, and bracing was added to keep the walls straight. The floor was sanded and varnished with polyurethane to a smooth and glossy finish. A new roof secured the renovation. While working on the barn, Bernie found part of a date scrawled on one of the rafters, indicating the barn was over a hundred years old. The last task was to stain the weathered wood. It seemed doubtful that it had ever been stained before; the siding absorbed forty gallons of stain ★

The renovated barn is now used to store equipment, including two restored, seventy-five-year-old tractors and a workshop on the lower level. The rebuilt second floor has held parties, including a wedding reception, and is enhanced with memorabilia affixed to the walls. When his barn was selected to represent the county, Bernie wasn't too sure what he thought of having a painting on the barn. He had always liked it looking just the way it was, but no one was prouder on the day it was dedicated ★

As Bernie worked on his restoration projects, he developed the idea of putting the valley back to the way it was seventy-five years ago. When other homes in the area went up for sale, the Fiedeldeys purchased and restored them. One of their daughters now lives in the old Bachmann farmhouse. Two other children live in houses just down the road. Someday it will be up to them to be the caretakers of the valley. As Bernie put it, this was his way of saving a piece of history for the township. The barn has stood for over one hundred years. He hopes it will stand for another hundred years. Some things, he feels, are better left unchanged ★

OWNER
Parminder and Polly Sandhu

LOCATION
20442 US Route 224, east of Findlay

The Hancock County barn has been a part of the landscape for over one hundred years. Although it no longer is part of a large working farm, it serves as a reminder of the county's agricultural heritage. Barn owners Parminder and Polly Sandhu are not farmers. When they purchased the property, east of Findlay, they were city folk harboring the desire for country life. Charmed by the old barn on the property, they were determined to preserve it for as long as possible. Their efforts were rewarded when the Bicentennial Commission selected the Sandhu barn to represent Hancock County ★

The county, formed in 1820, was named for John Hancock of the Revolutionary Congress. It was settled gradually; by 1830 the population was listed at only 813 people. One early settler was Jabab Wiemer, who purchased 160 acres of land from the United States government. The patent deed, dated March 15, 1836, was signed by Andrew Jackson ★

The property remained in the Wiemer family until 1929, when it was sold to James and Joseph Thomas. In 1936, the Thomases signed a land contract with Clifton and Elizabeth Vermillion. The Vermillions fulfilled the terms of the agreement and were awarded the deed to the property, dated April 12, 1943 ★

Otto Coffman and his family purchased the farm on October 28, 1949. They made several changes to the property. The old farmhouse was torn down and replaced with a modern home in 1964. A new foundation was put under the barn, but the inside was left unchanged and still has the original wood floor. The barn has hand-hewn beams and a frame joined by mortise and tenon construction. Small trees, still visible, were cut to provide additional supports ★

Parminder and Polly Sandhu purchased the farm from the Coffmans in 1992. Only five acres remain of the original farm, but it is enough for the Sandhus. They enjoy living away from the noise of the city and delight in the pleasures of country living. The family is proud to own Hancock County's Bicentennial Barn and look forward to Ohio's birthday celebration ★

Hardin

OWNER
Mark, Lance, and Kirk Shepherd

LOCATION
9430 State Route 309, in Kenton

In 1999, before the Shepherd barn was chosen to represent Hardin County, the family considered what they should do with the structure. It was old, needed work, and was used only for storage. In short, it had become a liability. The three owners, brothers Mark, Lance, and Kirk, decided the time had come to either restore or demolish it. Enter Beth Hansen, Bicentennial coordinator of Ohio's northwestern counties. Not sure exactly what they were in for, the Shepherd brothers agreed to let Scott Hagan use one end of their barn as a huge canvas. Many brushstrokes later, the Shepherd barn became Hardin County's Bicentennial Barn ★

In 1966, when Willis H. Shepherd purchased the farm, the 160 acres were tenant-farmed by the Beech family. They tended the land and used the barn for their dairy cows. The barn was built in the 1920s or 1930s to replace an older barn. Situated closer to the road, it had been lost to a fire ★

The Beeches lived for many years on the property and raised a family in the farmhouse. The oldest part of the house, built with small rooms, doors with transoms, and few, if any, closets, dates to the 1920s or earlier. An addition to the rear of the house was constructed about the same time as the newer barn. There was no modern plumbing. Water came from a cistern, and drinking water was carried to the house by hand. Heat was provided by a single oil stove ★

Shepherd and his sons made many improvements to the house and property. The brothers belonged to 4-H, and as they were growing up they kept calves in the barn. After Willis Shepherd's death, son Mark moved into the farmhouse. The Shepherds sold all but ten acres of the farm and expanded the trucking business their father started when they were young. Now called Cessna Transport, the company hauls hazardous materials in tankers and has flatbed trucks for moving steel and other large products ★

The Shepherds have worked on their barn ever since it was painted with the Bicentennial logo. Each year, area Amish boys are hired to work on the structure, and each year, something has been updated or changed. The barn now sports a new roof, new windows, new doors on new tracks, and steel siding on three sides. Mark Shepherd hopes to re-side the logo end of the barn, cut in new windows, and have painter Scott Hagan return to give him a fresh logo. Pride of ownership runs high in the family. The property is well maintained and landscaped, including house, barn, grounds, and outbuildings. Tons of gravel were recently put down to level and grade the many drives in and around the buildings ★

Committed to preserving the barn, the brothers are now looking to put it to good use. Currently, a horse and a pig occupy the barn, but they will have company in the future. Mark's son will soon have 4-H projects, so the Shepherds have turned their attention to the inside of the barn. They plan to use half of the barn for storage and the other half for livestock. The Shepherd brothers no longer talk about tearing down the old building. The Hardin County Bicentennial Barn is here to stay ★

Harrison

OWNER
Harrison County Commissioners

LOCATION
US Route 250, west of Cadiz

For the residents of the Harrison County Home, the painting of the Bicentennial logo on their barn was the highlight of the summer of 2001. They weren't used to having so many visitors all at once. Many barns in the county were nominated, and the regional coordinator finally narrowed the choice to two. Still undecided, she turned to the fourth and fifth grade classes at Jewett Elementary School. The students held an election and voted for the barn at the County Home. The residents were thrilled ★

Built in the 1930s, the barn replaced an earlier structure. Sitting on 380 acres, the barn was used by the residents of the home to shelter their livestock: cattle, sheep, chickens, and hogs. Back then, there were over one hundred people living at the home, and they were quite self-sufficient ★

Everyone worked to support themselves, and they had to follow the rules. Residents were required to take a bath once a week, be in bed by eight o'clock, and could receive company only on Sunday. They grew their own vegetables, and what they didn't eat they canned or took into town to the market. Those who didn't have a green thumb or a way with animals, mined coal used on the property ★

The first county home was built on the property in 1870, but burned down in 1904. Whatever was not destroyed was reused when the new home was built over the old foundation. The second home resembled the first, with broad steps leading to an imposing entrance. Some modifications were made, such as the addition of a second bell tower ★

A photograph of the old home hangs on the wall in the front entry hall of the new home. The long hallway leads to a rotunda, which is used as a sitting area. From each floor, an open circular balcony allows residents to hear or view entertainment below, or gaze at the spectacular, stained glass dome above ★

Times have changed at the home. The forty-one current residents no longer farm the land. They rely on government funding for necessities but depend on donations for extras. Recently, a large donation went to purchase new, comfortable furniture for the rotunda, giving it a warm and homey look ★

There are many other buildings on the property, some original to the farm, including the corncrib and smokehouse. At one time, there was an infirmary for residents who were difficult to control, but that was torn down in the 1970s. All buildings have been maintained and are used for storage ★

The barn sits high on a hill overlooking the surrounding countryside, a testimony to barn builders who selected sites that would provide good drainage. The residents of the Harrison County Home are justifiably proud of their barn. They were delighted with the festivities surrounding the painting and dedication and brought their lawn chairs to watch. Visitors to the property are welcome, and a kind word or wave will go a long way to brighten someone's day ★

Henry

OWNER

Marvin and Nancy Michaelis

LOCATION

9477 County Road O and US Route 6, in Napoleon

On July 2, 1999, a beaming Bernhard Michaelis accepted his birthday present from Scott Hagan: the official Henry County Bicentennial Barn, complete with logo and signed by the artist. Surrounded by family and friends, Bernhard celebrated his ninety-second birthday. Even he would admit it was one of the more unusual presents he had ever received, but few had made him prouder. His barn represented fifty-six years of commitment, dedication, and just plain hard work that began in 1943 when he first acquired the farm ★

The nation was in the middle of World War II when Bernhard and Edna Michaelis bought the farm on the edge of Napoleon. The purchase, made May 8, 1943, showed hope and optimism at a time the country was making unparalleled sacrifices for the war effort. They acquired the fifty-acre farm, on old Route 6, from John and Ruth Bostelman. The property had had a succession of owners, few owning it for more than ten years ★

The first recorded purchase of eighty acres was made in 1837 to James Wadsworth from the United States government. In 1907, Fred Lust bought the property, by then reduced to fifty acres, and sold it in 1918. It is believed he built the house on the property in 1915 and the barn the following year. The Bostelmans acquired the farm in January of 1943 and sold it a few months later to the Michaelises ★

Marvin Michaelis, one of Bernhard's five children, likes to say his father paid for the farm with cabbages. The Michaelis children, three sons and two daughters, helped their parents plant five to twelve acres of cabbage, done the old fashioned way by sowing seeds. They were, as Marvin jokes, the migrant workers of their day. The cabbage was packed into fifty-pound bags and shipped by truck to be sold in Cincinnati. The family also grew two to five acres of tomatoes, along with strawberries and pumpkins, which Edna sold at their roadside stand in front of the farm ★

The Michaelises kept at least sixty hogs, twelve to fourteen milk cows, and raised broilers and poulets. They grew corn, wheat, and oats to feed their livestock, seldom needing to purchase any feed. There were numerous outbuildings on the property, including a woodshed, a glazed brick milk house, hog sheds, and chicken coups. Two of the coops were portable; they could be hooked by a trailer and moved to a different lot on the farm, giving the chickens a change of scenery and something new to eat ★

In 1950, Bernhard began remodeling the old farmhouse. He removed plaster, rewired the walls, added new insulation, varnished the woodwork, and refinished the floors. That task completed, he started on the barn in 1953. About twenty feet of space was added to the east end of the structure, and the wood and dirt floor was replaced with concrete. A family effort, they mixed, poured, and troweled the concrete mixture themselves. In addition to replacing the floor, they created a new concrete feeding trough that ran the entire length of the stalls and curved up at the edges ★

The year 1958 saw more changes. The family raised thousands of broiler chickens and decided it was time for a new coup. Marvin, his father, and one of his brothers built one that measures forty by eighty feet, and to keep it always looking nice, they varnished the whole interior. Later that year, they added a two-car garage to the farmhouse. In 1962, Bernhard increased the size of his farm by buying an additional thirty acres ★

Edna Michaelis passed away in 1993, and the family lost Bernhard one year after the barn was painted. Together, the five Michaelis siblings cleaned out house, garage, and barn and had a large estate sale. They agreed upon a price for the property, and Marvin and Nancy purchased the farm ★

Marvin admits the Michaelis family is sentimental about the farm. He still has his father's 1934 Farmall A tractor, and his brother owns the International Harvester tractor their father bought new in 1946. They were all determined to save a pear tree that was very small when they moved onto the property so many years ago. The fall after their father's death, the tree became so heavily laden with fruit that it split in half. Still adamant about keeping it, Marvin carefully pruned it. The other half of the tree fell over at the first strong wind ★

The Michaelises rent their old homestead and most of the acreage, but keep the barn for storage. They are involved in a windbreak program and have planted over 1,100 trees, in two rows, along approximately one-half mile of property. There are still woods on the property, which Bernhard chose to preserve for birds and wildlife. Marvin will not change his father's wishes. He and Nancy are proud to be the caretakers of the Michaelis farm, preserving his parents' dreams and keeping alive memories for their own three children and other family members to enjoy ★

Highland

OWNER
James and Valerie Setty

LOCATION
3099 US Route 62, in Hillsboro

Highland County was created from Ross, Adams, and Clermont Counties in 1805. The new county encompassed the high elevation between the Scioto and Little Miami Rivers: the highlands. Owned by James and Valerie Setty, the Highland County Bicentennial Barn can be found a few miles south of Hillsboro, the county seat ★

In 1975, the Settys purchased the six-acre farm, including a house and barn. Both structures were built in the 1920s and had been sadly neglected. Work on the house included completely rewiring it, adding outlets as needed, and insulating the hollow walls ★

A new foundation was necessary for the barn before any other work could be done. They arranged to have the barn jacked up, and the new foundation was poured. While waiting for it to set, a violent storm unexpectedly hit the area. The high winds moved the barn several inches, forcing workers to reposition it on the jacks before it could be put back in place. Once this was accomplished, the Settys arranged for a new roof and totally replaced the weathered siding on the south side ★

For many years, the family raised tobacco, which they dried in the barn. Now it is used only for storage. When they heard the Bicentennial Commission was looking for a barn to represent the county, they considered offering theirs. Before they could complete the necessary paperwork, someone from the regional office came to their door asking if they would like to be a part of the project. The Settys were delighted. They take great pride in keeping the barn and grounds spotless, appropriately decorated for the season, and welcoming for all who come to visit ★

Hocking

OWNER
Regina and Sherman Prater

LOCATION
State Route 33 and County Road 10,
in Good Hope Township

Members of the Windy Hill Golf Club have driven past the barn for years. Few paid attention to the weathered, old structure tucked between the club entrance and the highway. Motorists traveling north on State Route 33 didn't take much notice, either. However, the barn made a lasting impression on one person ★

Nichola Moretti, the Bicentennial's southeast regional coordinator, used to traverse State Route 33 in her commute from school in Columbus to her home in Meigs County. Her journey was half over when she reached the Praters' barn. When it became time to choose a barn for Hocking County, there was no doubt which one she wanted ★

Regina and Sherman Prater purchased 300 acres of the former Andy Risch farm in 1982. They are now down to 250 acres, which includes the Bicentennial Barn, the golf club, three other barns, and a turn-of-the-century house, never improved with electricity ★

The property is on the outskirts of the village of Rockbridge, formerly known as Millville. Near the Hocking River, for which the county is named, the tiny town had a population of 250 in 1888 and was a stop on the Columbus, Hocking Valley & Toledo Railroad. A spur from the railway ran behind the barn, and old Route 33 lined up next to it. Traces of both can still be found, although Route 33 was relocated in 1937 ★

The bank barn was built around 1920 and still has the overhang from the second level, which has been removed from so many barns of similar construction. The barn was used to shelter cattle raised on the farm and for the storage of hay. The Risch family also raised hogs and grew corn and wheat. The barn is now retired from agricultural use and is used by the Praters for miscellaneous storage ★

Collectors of Bicentennial Barn trivia will note the logo was first painted on the barn in 1998 and included the outline of the state. When the barn was repainted in 2002, the state was covered over and only the logo remains. Spruced up for the state's 200th birthday celebration, the barn welcomes the many visitors to the parks and caves of historic Hocking County ★

Holmes

OWNER
Holmes County Commissioners

LOCATION
7260 State Route 83, in Holmesville

The Holmes County barn is nestled amid rolling, green hills and fertile farmland on the grounds of the Holmes County Home. The setting is both peaceful and quaint and provides the home's residents pleasing views from their windows. On warm days, a spacious veranda is the perfect place to relax and contemplate the countryside. Due to modern-day public health laws, residents don't have much else to do. That wasn't always the case ★

In 1866, Holmes County built an infirmary for the soldiers returning home from the Civil War. Many were ill or mentally unstable and were without resources to provide for themselves or family to care for them. The three-story building, with its broad porch on the south side, was said to be the pride of the county for many years ★

On the 320-acre site, a barn and numerous outbuildings were also constructed. The residents helped on the farm, raising potatoes, sweet corn, and other vegetables. They canned what they grew and in the spring tapped the abundant sugar maples to make maple syrup ★

A herd of cattle provided milk and butter for the home, and the sale of milk provided additional income. The milk was stored in cans at the nearby milk house, which is still standing. Cold water, used to refrigerate the milk, came from a well across the street and was pumped to the milk house by a windmill ★

In 1895, the home was destroyed by a fire, possibly caused by a defective flue in the kitchen chimney. All fifty-four residents escaped unharmed and watched as their home went up in flames. The building was replaced in 1870, and the bricks used in its construction were manufactured on the premises ★

The barn has been well maintained with very few changes. It continues to shelter cattle, as it has for more than one hundred years. Many of the outbuildings remain, although they are primarily used for storage. Each is labeled with an explanation of its original purpose ★

Residents farmed the land until the mid-1990s, when state food and health regulations prevented them from continuing to grow their own food. The property has been reduced to 290 acres. Both land and barn are now leased to a farmer ★

The residents, who used to watch their vegetables grow, now spend time watching television and doing crafts. Since the barn was dedicated as the Bicentennial Barn, they have found an additional form of recreation, that of watching the many visitors who stop at the barn and take photographs ★

Amish women, from Holmes County's thriving Amish population, come to the home once a week to work on quilts in the large, sunny activities room. Once a year, on the third Saturday in September, the County Home holds a huge auction of donated items, including the handmade quilts. Tourists who plan to view the barn, may want to schedule their visit to coincide with the auction. The residents will appreciate the support, and who knows what great buys are waiting ★

Huron

OWNER
Joe and Joann Sherman

LOCATION
479 US Route 250, in Olena

Surrounded by vast fields of grain, the Huron County Bicentennial Barn welcomes visitors who travel Highway 250, south of Norwalk. The county, formed in February of 1809, encompasses the area known as the Firelands. This land was granted to the State of Connecticut in 1792 to compensate for property loss that resulted from fire during the Revolutionary War. Norwalk, the county seat, takes its name from Norwalk, Connecticut ★

In 1856, Lewis Manahan purchased the farm in Olena. His daughter, Delia, married John Pratt, who operated a cheese factory with a partner, Edgar Tucker. The property stayed in the Pratt family for several generations ★

When Joe Sherman first saw the farm, it included a dilapidated carriage house, an aging farmhouse, and a barn. He rented the land from owners Leroy and Ethel Palm, hoping he would eventually be able to buy the entire farm. In 1974, Joe and Joann Sherman took ownership of the 161-acre farm ★

The house was built in 1850, and although there was a second story, it had no walls or ceiling. The Shermans prepared to totally renovate the Pratt homestead. They added new electrical wiring, replaced plumbing, tore off layers of linoleum, refinished floors, and gave the house a proper upstairs ★

About 1928, John Pratt built the barn on the property. The previous barn, built in 1904, was lost to fire. Joe built a new ramp to the main floor, resided the west end, replaced the roof, and did miscellaneous repairs. The lower floor of the barn was partially dirt, the rest was paved. Joe poured a new concrete surface over the entire floor and then built pens for the hogs he was planning to raise ★

One of the most humorous events he can recall came about because of a hog. Curious animals, one of them became fascinated with an old tire and tried (perhaps on a dare?) to walk through it. Predictably, he got stuck: two legs on one side, two on the other. No one knows how long he stumbled around the yard wearing his inner tube, but he was eventually spotted and rescued ★

Presently, the farmland is leased to the Shermans' son, who grows corn, soybeans, and wheat, and the remodeled farmhouse is used as rental property. The red, gambrel-roof barn, which measures thirty-six by sixty-five feet, is used for storage. Future plans call for restoration of the old carriage house ★

Joann Sherman and her daughter-in-law hold an annual barn sale and flea market. Popular with the community, it draws a large crowd of bargain seekers. In 2003, their signs and advertising will say, quite simply, that the sale will be held in the Huron County Bicentennial Barn ★

The Shermans became interested in the painting project after Joe Sherman saw an advertisement in *Ohio Farmer* about the Bicentennial Barns. He and Joann decided their barn met the necessary criteria and submitted the paperwork. They were pleased to be chosen to represent their county and happily welcomed those who gathered to watch the painting and subsequent dedication of the barn. Joe and Joann Sherman are proud to be the owners of the Huron County Bicentennial Barn ★

Jackson

OWNER
Paul and Mamie Lloyd

LOCATION
2401 State Route 93, in Oak Hill

A number of years ago, much like a modern day Brigadoon, Hitchcock's community came back to life for one day. Former neighbors returned from states as far away as Tennessee. They had all grown up together, back in the days of neighborhoods. Mamie Clark Lloyd recalls it as a wonderful time to be a child. A time when everyone looked out for one another and offered encouragement and support when things were tough. The Clark/Lloyd barn, long a fixture in the community, provided a familiar backdrop for the little neighborhood's event. Today, Jackson County's Bicentennial Barn proudly represents the little valley, once known as Hitchcock ★

Hitchcock derived its name from the general manager of a brickyard in nearby Oak Hill. The heavy clay, unique to the area, was perfect for manufacturing firebricks, bricks strong enough to withstand the high temperatures used in blast furnaces. The prosperity of the area was directly tied to the prosperity of the business, and the town of Oak Hill flourished, as the brickyard became a major employer ★

Mamie Lloyd grew up in the valley, largely settled by the Welsh. Her grandfather, Dr. John W. Clark, was a country doctor, who also built houses in the area. Her father, Turley L. Clark, became a teacher and principle at a local school. It was his dream to settle down and have a farm he could come home to at night. He designed the barn and hired Jim Walker to build it in the early 1940s. Clark kept horses, cattle, and even peacocks on the property ★

Turley Clark combined his love of the land with his love for children and teaching. Long before guidance counselors became popular, Clark took troubled children home with him, showing them what family life should be like and letting them help on the farm. Mamie was an only child but says she never thought about it because she was never alone. Clark passed away in 1958, at the age of fifty-five, and Mamie and Paul took over the farm ★

The barn used to provide a home for a herd of Brown Swiss cattle, but now it stores equipment used on the property. The Lloyds have made few changes to the barn, most notably, the color; the barn used to be white ★

They volunteered for the barn-painting project and waited hopefully during the selection process. Mamie was overcome with pride and emotion when her father's barn was finally chosen. She knows how thrilled he would be to have his barn represent the valley he loved and the county he grew up in ★

Owning a Bicentennial Barn was a perfect fit for Mamie and Paul. They both love people and have enjoyed meeting residents from counties all over the state. History lovers, they are happy to exchange information and find it interesting to learn little known facts about Ohio. Mamie is proud of her heritage and determined to preserve her father's farm. She and Paul are happy to share their barn with Ohio as it celebrates its Bicentennial ★

Jefferson

OWNER
Mary Grafton

LOCATION
1730 State Route 213, in Steubenville

It seems appropriate that the barn chosen to represent Jefferson County would be located in the city of Steubenville. After all, both county and city were named for patriots. The county, whose name honors President Jefferson, was created in 1797. Jefferson was the fifth county to be established in Ohio, extending from the Cuyahoga River, near Lake Erie, to the Ohio and Muskingum rivers. Steubenville began as Fort Steuben, which bore the name of Baron von Steuben, a drillmaster in the Revolutionary War. Von Steuben is credited with initiating a training program for soldiers ★

Steubenville, situated high above the Ohio River, was incorporated in 1805. One of its early settlers, Joseph Robertson, purchased property in a picturesque valley. There, in 1834, he built a one-and-a-half-story home, using money from the sale of one year's crop of potatoes. Joseph's son, a doctor, eventually located his practice in the house, using the two front rooms as an office and a waiting room ★

James W. and Ella B. Grafton purchased the farm from Dr. Robinson in 1898. For the next half-century, they operated a dairy business on their seventy-two acres of property. Their son, Craig, continued the tradition after Ella's death in 1956. He spent the rest of his life on the farm where he was born, and with his wife, Mary, raised six children in the Grafton farmhouse ★

Mary sold the dairy herd after Jim's death and now keeps a few head of beef cattle. Approximately one third of the acreage is devoted to pasture, and hay is the farm's primary crop. Mary believes her barn was built by the Robinson family, probably around the same time as the house. The original foundation was of wood and stone, but was undermined by groundhogs. The barn now has a new foundation of concrete block. The dirt floor in the lower level was also upgraded to concrete, and half of the slate roof was replaced with metal ★

The house on the property also deserves mention. Built in the Gothic Revival style, it has a centered gable, decorated with vergeboards, and a wide front porch. Entering the home provides a window to the past. The house has been well maintained, but renovation has been kept to a minimum. Wide, dark-stained moldings enhance rooms with high ceilings. Hiding behind tall doors, each room has at least one clothes press: shallow spaces with hooks designed for hanging a few items of clothing ★

Mary is proud of her historic property and is pleased to have her barn play a part in Ohio's Bicentennial celebration. She feels it is an honor for the Grafton family, and for the community, to represent Jefferson County. The dedication drew over a hundred people to the farm, including Mary's two brothers who live out of the area. The Grafton barn has received attention ever since. It has been painted and photographed by amateurs and professionals alike, and a local student created a model in miniature. Recently the barn was painted for publications of the Wild Turkey Association. Mary wishes her husband could have lived long enough to share in the excitement. A patriot and a lifelong farmer, he would have been proud to own the Jefferson County Bicentennial Barn ★

Knox

OWNER
Raymond and Dixie Luzader

LOCATION
7848 Columbus Road, west of Mount Vernon

Raymond and Dixie Luzader returned to Knox County in the 1980s. They had grown tired of urban sprawl and longed for the rural environment both had known in their youth. After selling their horse farm near Columbus, the Luzaders purchased a thirty-four-acre farm in Liberty Township. The property included an old house, a few outbuildings, and a weathered barn. Today that barn, patched and painted, welcomes visitors to Knox County as the Luzaders' Bicentennial Barn ★

The first settlers of Liberty Township came from Washington County, Pennsylvania. In 1805, they established themselves on the banks of Dry Creek, which runs through the Luzader farm. The first frame house was constructed on the property by Francis Atherton in 1808. Atherton's child was the first to die in Liberty township and was buried in the woods north of his home. Atherton also built a mill near the creek. Designed to be a gristmill, it was left uncompleted at his death ★

The barn on the farm was built in 1860, just before the start of the Civil War. The three-story structure was constructed with lumber sawn by a circular blade, probably from a local mill. The barn has several special features, including a corncrib built inside and doors cut into the floor of the second level. The doors, outfitted with handmade rings to pull up on, are for the purpose of dropping hay or feed to the animals below ★

Before the Luzaders acquired the farm, the house had been used as rental property. Raymond, a finish carpenter, began an extensive remodeling project. The house, now completely updated, has been personalized with his touches. There is new woodwork throughout, including moldings and doors, all designed and created by Raymond ★

In the barn he added foaling stalls on the upper level and regular stalls below. Recently he purchased old barn siding, so he can do repairs when needed. The barn still has its original slate roof and lightening rods, and the Luzaders hired men from the Amish community to repair and replace the gutters. The family is looking forward to again raising horses and seeing wobbly-legged foals in the barn ★

The Luzaders have an annual Halloween party with over a hundred people in attendance. They have hayrides on their property, pumpkin carving contests, and a large bonfire in the middle of the riding ring. Raymond and Dixie Luzader were pleased to have their barn selected to represent Knox County. They have enjoyed meeting people who stop to view their barn and are delighted when area grade schools bring classes to the farm to have their photographs taken in front of the barn. They expect 2003 to be a festive year and anticipate many visitors to their farm ★

Lake

OWNER
Dan and Linda Hearn

LOCATION
8249 Munson Road, in Mentor

It took a long time to find a barn to represent Lake County. Stretching along Lake Erie's coastline, the county was once dotted with farms and the summer homes of wealthy industrialists. In the 1900s, the county became well known for its greenhouses and nurseries. Many of them were headquartered in the city of Mentor ★

Originally a farming community, it became home to the rose-growing industry, producing close to 5 million plants a year. Mentor's rural atmosphere has changed, replaced by shopping malls, fast-food restaurants, and upscale housing developments. The barn chosen to represent Lake County stands as a symbol of Mentor's early years. Obscured from view by an overgrowth of shrubs, Dan and Linda Hearn's barn was just waiting to be discovered ★

The gambrel-roof barn has been in the Hearn family for four generations. Lizzie and Frank Parker, Dan Hearn's great-great-aunt and uncle, first purchased the twenty-five-acre farm in 1912. They raised cattle and hogs, and grew soybeans, timothy, and wheat. Dan's grandmother claims the Parkers made the best sausage in town ★

Eventually, the farm became the property of Dan Hearn's great-aunt and uncle, Ruth Carrig and Gilbert Kleeberger. Ruth worked at Wayside Gardens, one of Mentor's largest nurseries, and made perfume as a hobby; tucked away in a corner of the barn, the Hearns found boxes of the little bottles she used for her scents. Gilbert was the first Eagle Scouts master in the area and was in charge of Lake County's voting machines ★

The Kleebergers tore down the roomy, old farmhouse in the late 1940s and replaced it with a smaller home. They also demolished several outbuildings, including the outhouse. Dan has a comical photograph of Ruth leaning against the weathered, little building, pretending to push it over. Fortunately, Ruth and Gilbert did nothing to the barn ★

Aunt Lizzie and Uncle Frank circa 1920. Courtesy of Linda and Dan Hearn.

The three-bay threshing barn continues to stand, just as it was when first built. The large double doors, cut into each side, are suspended from the original track. A row of single-pane transom windows lines the top of each door. Horse stalls occupy one of the bays on the lower level, and the haymow still reaches to the rafters. The age of the barn has not been conclusively determined, but a small brass plaque attached to the siding indicates the lightening rods were installed in 1927 ★

Dan and Linda Hearn acquired the property, by then reduced to three acres, in 1998. Dan feels fortunate to have what is left of the farm but regrets his relatives didn't save the farmhouse. His childhood was spent in Madison, but he has many happy memories of family visits to the farm. Linda Hearn, who grew up in Willoughby, remembers passing the farm on the way to visit her relatives ★

One day, a representative from the Northeast Bicentennial office, Molly Randel, noticed the barn. It was difficult to see because of the trees in front of it, but she realized it was the perfect location for the Lake County barn. She approached the Hearns. They were thrilled at the prospect of being chosen, but dubious about having time or funds to repair rotted siding and clear away brush ★

After numerous telephone calls, the Lake County barn became a community project. A tree service company cleared the land of overgrown shrubs, and the barn, few people knew existed, was instantly visible. Paint, wood, and nails were donated to do repairs to the siding and prepare the barn for the logo. Volunteers power washed, primed, and painted the barn. A nursery delivered mulch, grass seed, and shrubs ★

The Hearns are proud and pleased their barn was chosen to represent Lake County. They had always hoped to save the barn and are now more determined than ever to preserve it. Dan's mother, Nancy Carrig Hearn, and his grandmother, Dorothy Carrig, joined them at the dedication in June of 2002. Linda and Dan, along with their two dogs, Caesar and Cleo, are happy to have visitors to their barn. They are looking forward to celebrating Ohio's Bicentennial ★

Lawrence

OWNER
Doris Higgins

LOCATION
4742 State Route 217, in Willow Wood

On a summer day in 2002, more than 400 people drove along the back roads of Lawrence County, each clutching a map published in an area newspaper. They drove past towns with names like Getaway and Polkadotte, along roads named Greasy Ridge and Bear Creek. Their objective was the small village of Willow Wood and the dedication of the Lawrence County Bicentennial Barn ★

In 1921, John and Nevada Barry moved their family from Gallia County to a new farm north of the Ohio River town of Proctorville. Moving day was May 1, and it began as a warm, sunny day, causing the family to remove their coats and throw them on the horse-drawn wagon with the rest of their possessions. As they headed south, they expected the temperature to rise, but, in fact, it did just the opposite. The coatless family nearly froze as a snowstorm blew in and blanketed the area ★

Barry family homestead.
Courtesy of Laversa Motes.

The superstitious might have considered the episode a negative sign, but the family prospered in their new home. John and his sons built a new dairy barn in 1925. His sons operated the Barry Brothers Dairy for many years, milking their cows by hand and storing the milk in large metal cans. They closed the dairy when sanitation regulations changed the way dairy farmers could do business. The Barry family felt they could not afford to modify their operation to conform to the new standards ★

After John's death, daughter Sylvia Thornton Watson moved her family to live with and care for Nevada. Sylvia's brother, Chancey, called Buck by family and friends, moved onto the farm when Nevada died. Brother and sister lived on the farm until Sylvia's daughter Jewell purchased it. In 1986, Jewell Roach sold the property to Paul and Doris Higgins ★

Paul and Doris made many changes to the farm. The farmhouse had fallen into disrepair and was torn down to make way for a modern log home. The barn was repaired, and a new roof secured it. The family kept the original lightening rods and hung the old hay hooks on the outside of the barn under the hay hood ★

For several years their animal collection caused motorists to stop for a second look. In time it became a petting zoo of sorts, and Paul Higgins started a day-in-the-country program for schoolchildren. Many children had never been on a farm and enjoyed seeing animals they only read about. In addition to livestock, the Higginses had a variety of other unusual animals such as llamas, peacocks, miniature horses, and emus ★

Cancellation created and provided by Earlein Meadows, Postmistress of Willow Wood.

Paul Higgins passed away in December of 2001. He loved people and enjoyed hosting large parties for the community. The Higgins family had read about the barn project, but Paul was convinced they would never choose his barn. The day the barn was dedicated, people began arriving early in spite of the rain. The event was well publicized; even the local post office got into the spirit by creating a special cancellation stamp for the day. Former owner Jewell Roach was there with her daughter, Laversa Motes. There was food, speeches, and buggy rides. All that was missing was Paul Higgins. "He would have loved it," said Doris ★

Licking

OWNER
Nelson and Kimberly Smith

LOCATION
*11641 Mount Vernon Road,
south of Utica*

The hundred-year-old barn looks oddly forlorn, as it sits alone in a small valley south of Utica. Once the center of activity on the farm, it is no longer filled with livestock; its stalls are empty, its doors are seldom open. Many visitors drive by the barn, ignoring it as they swarm to the Velvet Ice Cream Factory, a popular tourist attraction across the street. But thanks to the artistic talents of barn-painter Scott Hagan, the little barn has regained a sense of pride. Now adorned with a red, white, and blue logo, it is has become an equally popular attraction in the valley and is proud to be known as the Licking County Bicentennial Barn ★

Owned by Nelson and Kimberly Smith, the barn was built around 1900. Utica was experiencing a surge in population and prosperity at the turn of the century. Belgians, who had immigrated to the United States, settled in Licking and Knox counties and brought their glass-making skills with them. The New Utica Glass Factory was flourishing and providing employment for the town ★

In the year 1914, Velvet Ice Cream opened a factory in an old mill across the street from the barn. Although the current "old" mill is a reproduction, it was built over the original foundation. The site contains a museum, a restaurant, and, of course, an ice cream parlor ★

In the late 1960s or early 1970s, Joe and Juanita Stevenson took ownership of the twenty-eight-acre farm. The barn had received two additions in the early 1940s, greatly increasing its size. The Stevensons kept livestock, including sheep, in the barn, but their property was unfortunately located on a very sharp curve. There were frequent accidents, caused by people who failed to negotiate the turn. To avoid hitting another vehicle, the hapless motorists chose to plow right through the Stevenson fence line. Eventually, the family grew tired of chasing their sheep all over neighboring farms. They removed the livestock and began to use the barn for storing hay ★

Nelson Smith had wanted the farm for at least ten years. In 1984, he finally acquired it. Some time later, he divided the farm by selling twelve acres on the opposite side of the ravine. The barn is used for miscellaneous storage, and the acreage around it is left in a natural state ★

The Smiths are proud to say that their barn was featured on Governor Taft's 2002 Christmas cards. It has also appeared on the county road map and on a 2001 calendar distributed by the Park National Bank of Newark. Nelson and Kimberly plan to preserve the barn for some time to come and are happy to be the owners of the Licking County Bicentennial Barn ★

Logan

OWNER
Bill and Cindy Shepard

LOCATION
14485 State Route 235,
in Lakeview

On their first date, Bill Shepard took his girlfriend, Cindy, to have lunch with his grandmother, Lottie Riebel. Bill had many fond memories of childhood days spent with his family, visiting his grandparents' farm. As he walked Cindy around Lottie's house and property, Bill introduced Cindy to her future home, but neither of them knew it then ★

Since 1939, Lottie and her husband, Harvey, were the owners of the fifty-nine acre farm in the small community of Lakeview. They purchased the property from a family named Jacobs, who owned most of the nearby town of Avondale. The Riebels raised a wide assortment of animals on their property, including dairy cattle, horses, sheep, pigs, peacocks, chickens, ducks, and geese. Bill's mother, and her brother and sister, grew up on the farm playing in the hayloft and swinging on the ropes, all under the watchful eyes of their border collie, Frosty ★

Harvey Riebel passed away in the late 1960s. Lottie continued to live on the farm for the next twenty years, trying her best to look after her animals and do the necessary maintenance. Her grandson came to visit often until her death in 1988. Bill's uncle bought the farm from Lottie's estate and moved into the farmhouse. Over the next nine years, he and his son turned the house into somewhat of a warehouse, raising rodents they sold to pet stores. After setting up an incubator in the kitchen, they moved into a house across the street ★

In August of 1997, Cindy and Bill moved their family into the house, airing it out and making extensive repairs. The house had no central heating system, and the electricity was barely adequate. They officially purchased it in 1998. While working on the house, they found the date June 1903 carved into one of the blocks around the front porch. Until then, no one had been able to approximate the age of the house ★

Once the house was comfortable, they started work on the barn. They tore out what they didn't need, patched the foundation, and replaced some of the siding. Horses now occupy half of the barn, and during the winter months, the other half shelters their flock of sheep. The spacious loft has room for five to six hundred bales of hay ★

One day, Cindy found herself driving in an unfamiliar area and pulled out an Ohio map to get her bearings. Intrigued by the photograph of a Bicentennial Barn on the map, she called to find out more about the program. The Shepards' barn was selected not long after Cindy submitted a letter and photograph. Family and friends surrounded Cindy and Bill, and their children: Tyler, Lynsey, and Haley when the barn was dedicated. They all agree that having a Bicentennial Barn is "cool" and enjoy sharing their part of Ohio's history with visitors ★

Lorain

OWNER
Gerald and Janet Eschtruth

LOCATION
9455 State Route 58, in Amherst Township

Lorain County's Bicentennial Barn is located on busy State Route 58, south of the city of Amherst. Owned by Gerald and Janet Eschtruth, it is situated close to the heavily traveled road, which connects the southern towns of Wellington and Oberlin with the Ohio Turnpike and the larger cities of Elyria and Lorain to the north. The red and white barn sits as a staunch reminder of a time when miles of fields separated neighbor from neighbor, town from town ★

The Eschtruths acquired the twenty-nine acres of property, including the barn and farmhouse, in 1997. They don't know who built the barn but believe it was constructed between 1915 and 1920. In the 1930s and 1940s, Dick Gergel operated a poultry business on the farm. Sometime after World War II, the property was purchased by Harold Gage, who raised beef cattle and hogs ★

Ralph and Dorothy Thomas took ownership of the farm in the 1960s. Ralph was a machinist and set up his small business in a portion of the barn. The Thomases started a second business, a trap-shooting club they called the Route 58 Gun Club. They used the vacant part of the barn as the clubhouse, offering food and beverages and equipping it with picnic tables for their customers ★

Gerald and Janet Eschtruth use the barn for storage and rent out the farmhouse. The land is still farmed; corn and soybeans are the primary crops. The Eschtruths plan to preserve their barn and are exploring alternative uses, such as an antique shop or lawn mower repair business. They were surprised when approached about the barn-painting project but were pleased to be chosen. To get ready for the Bicentennial celebrations, they painted the entire barn and made repairs to the old slate roof. History is important to the Eschtruth family, and they are proud to represent Lorain County ★

Lucas

OWNER
Josephine Meeker

LOCATION
1625 S Crissey Road, in Monclava

John Carpenter looked forward to strawberry-picking days. The whole family was invited to help and later gathered to picnic on his farm. In those days, traffic drove slowly past Uncle John's fruit and vegetable stand, located near the two-lane road at the front of his property. Patiently he sat with his cane, waiting for customers. His relatives continue to treasure memories of those peaceful days fifty years after his death. John Carpenter loved his farm and would be proud to know that his barn was chosen as the Lucas County Bicentennial Barn ★

In the late 1800s, John and Lillie Carpenter purchased acreage in rural Monclava. A small creek ran through the property, parallel to the main road. As was often the case, John built a barn first and then began work on a new house, which he completed in 1897. Leonard Meeker, John's nephew, moved from Grand Rapids, Michigan, to live with his aunt and uncle. It was his responsibility to look after the huge strawberry patch and care for the cows, chickens, and horses ★

Leonard and his wife, Josephine, became owners of the farm when Uncle John passed away in the mid-1950s. They already owned a house in Toledo, but Leonard was fond of the farm and wanted to keep it. The decision was made to spend summers in the country and return to the city in time for school in the fall ★

The Meeker family was a large one, with six sons and five daughters. Josephine made jelly and canned food for the family to eat during the winter. There was a large orchard, which produced peaches, apples, grapes, and raspberries. An expansive garden yielded potatoes, corn, tomatoes, and other vegetables, all of which they sold at a stand set up in Uncle John's old barn ★

Built to last a lifetime, the barn measures thirty by forty feet, and is thirty-two feet high. It has hand-hewn beams and is joined by mortise and tenon construction with wood pegs. The well-maintained barn has double arches painted on its doors, a feature once popular on barns in the Midwest. At one time a Mail Pouch Tobacco sign adorned the rear of the barn. Still attached to the barn siding is a Mail Pouch thermometer, which continues to accurately display the temperature ★

Although Leonard Meeker passed away twenty years ago, the family continues to manage the four-acre farm. They rent the old farmhouse and use the barn to store equipment needed on the property. One of Josephine's sons cuts grass and does repairs around the farm; another son works at the market just across the street. The road in front of the farm is now the multi-laned Airport Highway; the creek was paved over when the road was widened. Land on all sides of the property is zoned for industrial use, and neighboring farms are for sale ★

The Meeker family still goes to the farm for picnics, although traffic rushing down the highway has created a different atmosphere. Nevertheless, each year they make a point of gathering to celebrate Josephine's birthday. Everyone, including her grandchild and great-grandchild, returns to the farm for the party. It is a time to pay tribute to Uncle John and Aunt Lillie and reminisce about childhood summers spent with their father. The Meekers are proud of their family history and pleased to own Lucas County's Bicentennial Barn ★

Madison

OWNER
James and Regina Moats

LOCATION
Interstate 71, in Mount Sterling

With a mixture of dread and excitement, the early settlers of Madison County looked forward to the livestock drovers' arrival. They came on horseback and on foot, and moved cattle, sheep, and hogs along the Federal Road. As they progressed from Pittsburgh, Pennsylvania, to Peoria, Illinois, they stopped at towns and farms along the way. They were greeted with enthusiasm, for they brought news and tall tales, and they had money to spend ★

The drovers considered a small town in Madison County to be their halfway point. Its official name was Sedalia, but they named it, appropriately, Midway. The crossroads community prospered, adding a hotel, saloons, stores, and businesses that catered to the drovers' every need. After celebrating completion of the first half of their journey, the group moved on. As they kicked up the dust on Federal Road, they passed the Chenoweth barn. It is now owned by James and Regina Moats and stands proudly as Madison County's Bicentennial Barn ★

The Chenoweths were a pioneer family who assembled a large farm near Mount Sterling. They fell upon poor economic times and sold the 350-acre farm to John and Ellen Moats in 1904. The farm is now owned by their grandson, Jim, who finds traces of early farming days when he plows his fields and turns up horseshoes. Jim grew up in the area and married Regina Timmons, who was born and raised on the Federal Road, now State Route 323. Regina's great-great-grandfather, Lewis Timmons, was the first mayor of Mount Sterling, elected March 12, 1842. Regina Timmons Moats is the seventh generation to live in Madison County ★

The Moats barn was built in 1840. The timber frame is oak, joined by mortise and tenon construction. The barn was used to stable draft horses, which the family raised. There are four tie stalls on the west end and three box stalls on the east for mares and colts. The interior of the barn appears exactly as it was when built; there have been no changes ★

The original foundation was made of huge logs, laid parallel to the ground. Over time they rotted through and began to destroy the pine siding. In the 1960s, the barn was jacked up, the logs removed, decayed siding cut off, and a new concrete foundation established. To prepare the barn for the Bicentennial, Jim Moats repaired the doors and painted the barn. It is used for storage of hay and straw ★

Jim and Regina Moats volunteered their historic barn to represent their county. They could hardly believe their luck at being selected and have become overnight celebrities. They take their responsibilities very seriously and delight in the media attention they have received. An ever-growing scrapbook bears testimony to their numerous public appearances and interviews. The barn was first dedicated on July 11, 1998, when the logo was painted on the west end of the barn. Scott Hagan returned in September of 2002, repainted the west end, and added the logo to the east end. Jim and Regina Moats and their dog, Zoe, welcome all visitors to their barn. They are proud to represent their county as the owners of the Madison County Bicentennial Barn ★

Mahoning

OWNER
Joyce Flowers

LOCATION
7435 Tippecanoe Road, in Canfield

The Mahoning County Bicentennial Barn sits on a hillside in Canfield, and overlooks the Ohio Turnpike. When seen from the highway, with its missing cupola, weathered siding, and crumbling foundation, it might appear to be just another sadly neglected barn. Closer examination reveals a very different story ★

With pride of ownership, Joyce Flowers has entered into the spirit of the Bicentennial and is determined to give Ohio a birthday barn it can be proud of. Throwing her considerable determination and energy into the project, Joyce is committed to a total restoration of her barn ★

The barn was once a part of Heberding Dairy, the largest dairy farm in northeast Ohio. The farm complex had several hundred acres of farmland, pastures, barns, outbuildings, tenant houses, and a large family residence. Some customers traveled quite a distance to purchase their milk, ice cream, and other dairy products fresh from the farm. The Heberding complex had its own sawmill and a powerhouse that produced 440 volts of electricity to power their generator ★

The Ohio Turnpike bisected the property in the 1950s, and soon the family closed the dairy. Land was later parceled and sold through a family trust. The original Heberding homestead is still standing, but it was separated from the farm and sold on an adjacent parcel of land ★

In the 1970s, Joyce Flowers bought what was left of the farm. Structures on her twenty-one acres included two barns, one too unstable to be saved, and several houses and outbuildings. She leased the land to a farmer and finally moved onto the farm in 1990. Joyce now lives in a former tenant house, which has been totally renovated ★

The Bicentennial Barn was built by the Amish in 1954, as a prototype barn. Framing resembles that of a house, with floor joists on sixteen-inch centers. Over time, a family of groundhogs elected to live under the barn and began creating a network of tunnels and burrows. It wasn't long before they undermined the foundation, and the barn began to list. The barn was placed on jacks and lifted so the old foundation could be removed. During the excavation, workers found burrows extending six feet into the earth ★

When restored, the barn will have a new foundation, a concrete floor, and a custom built cupola to replace the one blown off in a violent storm. The groundhogs have been encouraged to live elsewhere ★

Joyce Flowers is pleased to be part of the barn-painting project. She hopes her barn will serve as a symbol of preservation and a tribute to the hardworking dairy farmers of Ohio for many years to come ★

Marion

OWNER
Gerald and Bonita Schultz

LOCATION
*333 Prospect–Mount Vernon Road,
in Waldo*

In 1810, Nathaniel Wyatt opened a tavern near the present-day community of Waldo. Wyatt's Tavern was located on a road popular with early settlers traveling north and south through what was then Delaware County. The War of 1812 brought soldiers through the area that would later become Marion County. To protect settlers from attacks by Indians, a fort was erected around the tavern. Called Fort Morrow, it covered half an acre, had eight-foot high walls, and was anchored by two blockhouses. As Ohio prepared to celebrate its 200th birthday, they chose a barn near the site of the old fort and tavern to represent Marion County ★

The Bicentennial Barn is located on the Schultz farm in Waldo. The first owners of the property, as recorded in 1835, were the Kenyon family: Samuel and Eunice, Thompson and Indiann, and Daniel. In 1939, Clifford Graham purchased the farm. In the early 1970s, Gerald Schultz passed the farm on his daily drive to work. Each day he admired it and wondered if he would ever be able to call it his own. He soon found a way to work on the farm, and after four or five years, he made his dream come true ★

Gerald and Bonita Schultz purchased the 107-acre farm in 1976. They grow beans, wheat, corn, and hay on their acreage and raise Belgian draft horses. The Belgians have stalls in the barn, which is also used to store their hay and straw ★

The barn was built in the 1930s. It was formerly used as a dairy barn, but the cow stanchions have been removed and the silo torn down. Gerald had the roof replaced with standing-seam in the 1990s. One note of curiosity is the name carved into a beam in the haymow. It appears to be E K PRETZ, although the letters aren't as clear as they may once have been. It hasn't been determined if that is the name of the builder or perhaps someone who lived or worked on the farm ★

When the Schultz barn was selected to represent the county, Gerald made arrangements to paint the entire barn before Scott Hagan arrived to do his artwork. As Scott began to set up his scaffolding, the Schultzes watched with astonishment at the volume of people who descended upon their property. Cars started arriving early on the first morning and drivers parked on both sides of the road. As traffic increased, Gerald became concerned for visitors' safety and finally swung open the gates to his farm. In they spilled: cars, trucks, campers, and motorcycles. The couple is in agreement that the crowd was polite and friendly and, over the course of the two-day event, left not a single item behind. Gerald and Bonita Schultz are very proud to be the owners of the Marion County Bicentennial Barn ★

Medina

OWNER
John and Kathleen Swagler

LOCATION
8354 Wooster Pike Road, in Seville

Medina County was organized in 1818, on the heavily forested lands of Connecticut's Western Reserve. Early settlers, arriving on roads barely passable, cleared land for farms and built their barns. They quickly established Medina County as an agricultural center. The county seat was created in the city of Medina, and court was first held in a barn, just north of the present day courthouse ★

Today, Medina's historic public square has become a tourist attraction. The original buildings, now restored, are occupied by antique stores and coffee shops and surround the village green. Not far from town, the county's agricultural past is still apparent. Farms still cover the landscape with fields of colorful crops, peaceful pastures, and welcoming farmhouses. The Swagler Barn, a few miles south of Medina, was chosen to represent the county as Medina County's Bicentennial Barn ★

John and Kathleen Swagler have owned the Gothic-roof, sometimes called round-roof, barn since the late 1960s. There were once two barns on the thirty-eight acre farm, possibly dating to the 1800s. They both burned to the ground in a fire started by sparks from a threshing machine. The new barn was built between 1939 and 1940 as a dairy barn. It measures thirty-six by sixty-four feet ★

The Swaglers removed the cow stanchions and equipped the barn for the quarter horses their daughters raised for 4-H. Kathleen remembers the record-breaking winter of 1977-78, when the girls carried buckets of water to the barn through blowing and drifting snow. The temperature plummeted the night a colt was born, and Kathleen wrapped it in an old sweater to keep it from freezing to death. To everyone's great relief, the colt survived ★

The family resides in the 1848 homestead on the property. The restored farmhouse is a comfortable and modern home, with its architectural charm preserved. John and Kathleen do not farm their land, choosing instead to rent it to a local farmer. The barn is currently home to Austrian-bred mountain horses, called Haflingers. It is also used to protect the objects of John's hobby, two restored 1953, Allis Chalmers tractors. His first restoration project was the WD45, which belonged to Kathleen's father. His other tractor is a G model, with the motor in the back instead of the front ★

When the Bicentennial Commission advertised for a barn in Medina County, the Swaglers considered nominating theirs. They were delighted when the regional coordinator, Jennifer Bucci, stopped at the farmhouse and asked them if they would consider the project. John and Kathleen Swagler are proud to have their barn be a part of Ohio's Bicentennial celebration and look forward to greeting visitors to their farm ★

Meigs

OWNER

Horace and Dorothy Karr

LOCATION

State Route 7 and Flatwoods Road, northeast of Pomeroy

You can almost see the hundred-year-old barn shudder, as huge pieces of earthmoving equipment carve out a new road a hundred yards from its foundation. Three houses, all built at the turn of the twentieth century, all belonging to the barn's original owner, have been destroyed to make way for the excavation. The barn will be spared, however. Preservationists have seen to that, and it will stand, for at least for a few more years, as Meigs County's Bicentennial Barn ★

Frank Wells bought a hundred-acre farm around 1900. Frank and his wife, the former Emmaline Wickham, had three sons: Ivan, Floyd, and Clyde. Frank built the barn, with help from Ivan and Floyd, to provide shelter for his dairy cows and storage for corn, oats, and hay. Floyd moved to Zanesville, and Clyde and Ivan started families of their own ★

Ivan and Helen Wells purchased the 110-acre Warner farm next door and moved into a house on that property. Together, the Wells family farm totaled 260 acres. Ivan's daughter, Margaret Yost, grew up on the farm and worked with her father until her marriage. As an only child, she hauled manure, milked cows, worked in the garden, and drove a team of horses to pull hay ★

In addition to farming, the Wells brothers worked for friends who owned the Fensterwald Funeral Home. Fensterwald administered to the large German and Amish population in the area and transported coffins to numerous little cemeteries that dotted the hillsides. There was a long barn on the Wells property where the brothers kept the hearses and the horses required to pull them. They owned several vehicles, including a long cab used to transport the family. Both hearse and cab were black covered carriages, with darkened windows and lanterns on either side ★

In those days, bodies were not embalmed and were kept at home until the undertaker removed them to the church and cemetery. The brothers had to sit with the hearse in all kinds of weather. They bundled up in heavy overcoats during the winter, but donned the black coats and hats of their trade when weather permitted ★

Horace and Dorothy Karr eventually purchased the farm from the Wells family in 1966. Their son still farms the land, raising Red Angus cattle, and growing soybeans, hay, and corn. The barn is used for his horses and to store hay. The farm was recently divided, when the State of Ohio purchased seventy-six acres of the Karr farm to begin the construction of the new highway ★

The Karrs are very much interested in history and preservation. Dorothy Holter Karr, who descends from the Genheimer family, can trace her roots back to the county's origin. When she was a little girl she played the piano at a small German Methodist church near the Karrs' present home. High on a hill, overlooking the church, was a tiny cemetery, and Dorothy can remember looking out the church's narrow windows and seeing the mourners silhouetted against the sky. Not long ago, Horace and Dorothy purchased property including the church and cemetery. It is their plan to restore the church and preserve the cemetery ★

The Karrs are pleased and proud their barn was selected to represent Meigs County. Although disheartened by the loss of their property to the road construction, they will continue to maintain and protect the barn. They hope it will serve to remind future generations of the contributions early farmers made to the history of Meigs County ★

Mercer

OWNER
Todd and Dee Laux

LOCATION
7619 US Route 127, in Celina

The haymow is empty, the horse stalls are vacant, and cattle no longer graze the fields surrounding the Laux barn. Built over a hundred years ago, it has served many owners and experienced a variety of uses. After years of sheltering livestock, the barn was reduced to serving as a pickle factory. Subsequent owners manufactured furniture in the cavernous building. Still upright, it has been restored and proudly stands as the Mercer County Bicentennial Barn ★

Dee and Todd Laux purchased their three-and-one-half-acre farm in 1990. The previous owners, Sadie and Walder Sielschott, moved to the farm in the late 1940s or early 1950s. For many years, they rented from Harold Bowman, a wealthy businessman who owned several farms in the area. The Sielschotts grew wheat, oats, and corn and raised a herd of cattle ★

Eventually, Bowman sold his 120-acre farm to Sadie and Walder. Their son, Edgar, and his wife, Louise, purchased another Bowman farm just down the road. Edgar and Louise recall many good times spent in the farmhouse on his parents' farm. Louise remembers that Sadie was a great cook and worked wonders in the kitchen, cooking for family, friends, and everyone who worked on the farm. Edgar no longer actively farms, but he misses those days spent working with his father. To him, farming is about putting out crops, watching them grow, and being able to make a living doing what you love ★

Dee and Todd Laux are doing their best to preserve the farm the Sielschotts so fondly remember. They installed a new roof on the barn, replaced the west end with steel siding, and gave it a new coat of paint before the logo was painted. The old farmhouse has been renovated and will continue to provide a comfortable home for its occupants ★

The Laux family is pleased that their barn was chosen to receive the Bicentennial logo. Dee and Todd have four children, but only two are old enough to understand the significance of the barn painting and dedication. Hopefully, the experience will give the older children memories for a lifetime. They feel honored to be a part of Mercer County's history and extend a warm welcome to visitors who come to see their barn ★

Miami

OWNER
Fred and Brenda Copeland

LOCATION
4080 State Route 48, in West Milton

In 1998, Fred and Brenda Copeland first visited a six-acre farm for sale in West Milton. They were charmed by the old house, and they could see it had potential, but it was the white barn that won them over. The siding was missing in places, and the stone foundation was crumbling, but the massive beams, cut from huge trees long ago, held the structure together. They bought it. Thus began a restoration project the village could not ignore. Although the Copeland were newcomers, their dedication to the property was duly noted, and residents nominated the Copeland barn to represent Miami County as their Bicentennial Barn ★

As the Copelands worked on the house, they discovered items that intrigued them, such as a four-foot crawl space between the first and second floors. Brenda worked at researching the property in an effort to learn its history. The first record of sale shows eighty acres purchased in 1836 by Abner Vore, one of the original three settlers in the village of West Milton. The Vore family hired Weller Benton, from Darke County, to build a frame house on the their farm. In 1850, the home was valued at $135 ★

During the Civil War, W. B. Cox owned the farm. His son, Lloyd, stenciled his name and the date, July 1874, on a beam in the barn. The property, by then reduced to forty-four acres, remained in the Cox family until 1922. Descendants from many of the old families of West Milton still live in the area, and one woman told the Copelands that she walked past the farm every day on her way to school in 1912. She still remembers picking the lilies that grew near a spring on the Cox property ★

The old farmhouse remained virtually unchanged for nearly a hundred years. It was built with fourteen-foot ceilings, six fireplaces, a huge staircase, and thick wood moldings. In 1949, Herbert and Josephine Busse purchased the farm and extensively remodeled the house. The Copelands were told that the Busses' daughter married a war veteran and, as was often the case, could find no available housing. The Busses creatively lowered the ceilings to make an apartment on the second floor for the couple ★

The restoration project undertaken by the Busses resulted in the four-foot crawl space discovered by the Copelands. It was preserved as a time capsule of the home's previous decor. Brenda explored its entire length with her camcorder. She discovered the old wallpaper and bits of the ten-foot door and window frames ★

Susie

During the thirty-eight years the Busses owned the property, they raised Black Angus cattle, and chickens were kept in a large coop behind the barn. The Busses divided the farm and sold the present six-acre parcel in 1987. The property was purchased by Rick and Beth Myer, who sold it to the Copelands in 1998 ★

The Copelands felt that the barn needed immediate work if they were to save it. The foundation could be mortared over for strength, but they needed lumber to replace the rotted siding. Fred Copeland works for the Dayton News, and in a stroke of good luck, the company ordered new printing presses. The equipment was shipped from Austria in huge wooden crates made of two by six planks, exactly the size they needed. Fred dismantled the crates and brought the lumber home ★

The barn, now painted red, has a new floor, siding, and doors. The Copelands hold barn dances and give dance lessons to the community. Three acres of the farm are leased to a farmer who grows corn. They love living in West Milton and are proud they have been able to preserve a part of its early history. Fred and Brenda feel honored to own the Miami County Bicentennial Barn and plan to hold events on their property during 2003 ★

Monroe

OWNER
Mike and Beth Roberts

LOCATION
43038 Plainview Road, south of Woodsfield

Today, the small town of Griffith exists only on detailed atlases and in the memories of longtime residents of Woodsfield. In the early 1900s, the discovery of oil brought workers to the area and prosperity to its residents. The town had a one-room schoolhouse, gas station, delivery stable, and more than twenty saloons. Oilfield workers stabled their horses in Scott Higgins' new barn. When the workers left and the saloons closed, Griffith sank into obscurity. A recent event has brought renewed interest in the town, and visitors back to the area. In June of 2001, Scott Higgins' barn, which now belongs to Mike and Beth Roberts, was dedicated as the Monroe County Bicentennial Barn ★

Scott Higgins hired Charles Griffith to build a new barn for him in 1917. It went on the tax records of the county the following year. Scott's son, Ott, and his wife, Minnie, were the next owners of the farm, and they sold it to Brian Ludwig ★

In July of 1990, Mike and Beth Roberts purchased the house, barn, and five acres of land. One end of the barn had a faded advertisement painted in the 1930s. It was for the Bowser Sales and Trading Company. The business, which operated in Antioch and Sisterville, among others, sold feed for dairy cows and poultry ★

At the time, the Roberts knew very little about the barn, but it soon became apparent that residents of the area were very fond of it. Mike noticed a man who drove slowly by the house each day, fixing his gaze on the barn. Finally, he stopped and demanded to know what Mike was planning to do with the barn. Now, Mike hadn't really given much thought to that issue, but he assured the man that tearing it down was not a consideration ★

As others came forward with the same question, Mike and Beth turned their attention to repairing the barn. New windows were added shortly before two tornados touched down, ripping off one half of the roof and causing other damage to the property. The entire roof was replaced as a result ★

The former village of Griffith. Courtesy of Beth and Mike Roberts.

In the spring of 2000, Beth saw the logo painted on the Belmont County barn and began asking questions. She sent photos to the Bicentennial Commission but heard nothing for a very long time. In August of that year, she saw an advertisement in a local paper and resubmitted her photographs and application. Finally, in January 2002, she was contacted, and the barn was soon selected. When Scott Hagan painted the Bicentennial logo, he also repainted the Bowser sign ★

Mike and Beth Roberts grow hay on their five acres of land and use the barn for yard sales and storage. The barn-painting project has brought history to life for the Roberts children, Morgan and Micah. The family has made a series of trips to various counties in Ohio, visiting the Bicentennial Barns and stopping at historic sites in the area. They are proud to own Monroe County's barn, and are looking forward to the events of the Bicentennial year ★

Montgomery

OWNER
AIDA Technologies

LOCATION
Interstate 70W, in Huber Heights

Montgomery County was officially formed in 1803 and named for General Richard Montgomery of the Revolutionary War. The seat of justice was established in Dayton, a small village of five families, on the east bank of the Great Miami River. The population grew slowly until work began on the Miami-Erie Canal. In January 1829, with much fanfare, the first packet boat arrived in Dayton from Cincinnati ★

The canal brought commerce to the town, and it never looked back. Many companies had their first small beginnings in Dayton but grew into international corporations. National Cash Register was founded in 1886, Delco Engineering in 1910. Brothers Orville and Wilbur Wright put Dayton on the map with the invention of a flying machine. During World War II, the Dayton-Wright Airplane Company produced a more sophisticated version of the invention ★

As Dayton grew and corporate headquarters expanded, it was inevitable that farmland surrounding the city would be sold and developed. The barn chosen to represent Montgomery County was once part of a farm in Huber Heights. It now belongs to AIDA Technologies, a leading builder of metal forming and stamping presses ★

The barn was constructed by the Barr brothers: Harry, Newton, and Joseph. Well known in the area, they constructed hundreds of buildings between 1850 and 1920. Their barns were framed with a huge center bay, large enough to allow a team of four horses and hay wagon to turn completely around. They paid great attention to the exterior architecture of their buildings, and even barns received ornamental details. Windows, doors, and cupolas were designed to be attractive, as well as functional ★

The AIDA barn is a bank barn, with stables and livestock pens on the lower level and room for the storage of hay and grain on the upper level. The windows are arched and louvered, with herringbone patterned doors and round light portals ★

The twenty-acre farm was owned by Raymond McDonald for seventeen years. He used the barn for storage and rented out the house on the property. The oldest part of the house is approximately one hundred years old but has a newer addition. McDonald put time and effort into renovating the farmhouse, making improvements and updating it throughout. He purchased the farm from J. Armstrong, who farmed the land and raised hogs. In 1995, McDonald sold his farm to AIDA Technologies ★

AIDA has not made a decision about a future use for their historic barn. They are committed to preserving it as a tribute to the Barr brothers and to the farmers who settled Montgomery County 200 years ago ★

Morgan

OWNER
Don and Sheila Graham

LOCATION
5159 Barr Road, in McConnelsville

In 1895, Howard Chandler Christy, a little known artist from Ohio, created a cover for *The Century* magazine. The glamorous woman he depicted became known as the "Christy Girl," and her likeness appeared in his illustrations for books and magazines, as well as individual artwork. During World War I, Christy was commissioned to design posters for the Red Cross and United States Navy, and again he incorporated the image of his lady ★

Christy's work is considered highly collectible, and people occasionally make a pilgrimage to visit the site of his birth. In 1873, he was born on a farm in McConnelsville, now owned by Don and Sheila Graham. The foundation of his homestead is crumbling but still standing; the chimney has been reduced to rubble. Recently, the Grahams have noticed an increase in the visitors to their property. It all started when their big, red barn was dedicated as the Morgan County Bicentennial Barn ★

In 1969, the Grahams purchased the 200-acre farm from George and Gladys Hall. The Halls owned the property for more than twenty years, and they passed along its history with copies of old deeds and records. Don and Sheila live in a house on the property that actually predates the Christy birthplace. Their house was built in 1846 with bricks made on the farm ★

Although the house has been modernized, the Grahams have made few changes to their barn. Based on a dated cornerstone they found while working on the foundation, they believe it was constructed in 1891. At one time, the barn sported a Mail Pouch Tobacco logo, but a storm caused damage that removed any trace. The Grahams use the barn to shelter their cattle and a herd of goats. The addition was constructed using timber salvaged from an old barn on the property ★

Don and Sheila Graham are proud to own Morgan County's Bicentennial Barn. Their tidy farm sits high on a hillside, overlooking State Route 78, as it has done for over a hundred years. The historic house and barn have stood as mute observers to our progress. Today, they stand in tribute to Ohio's past ★

Morrow

OWNER
Harold, Kenneth and Elizabeth Bush

LOCATION
State Route 95, west of Edison

In 1857, when Laban Brown proudly built his barn in the little community of Edison, Morrow County was not quite ten years old. Mount Gilead, two miles down the road, was founded in 1824. Once part of Marion County, it became the seat of justice for the new county in 1848. Still very much pioneer land, the population was a mere 400. Brown was one of the first property owners in the new county ★

Laban Brown married the girl next door, Susannah Clevenger Bush. Upon his death in 1906, she inherited the farm. Her son, Will Bush, owned it from 1912 to 1928. The farm, owned by the family for over seventy years, was lost to them when Will Bush passed away. In 1929, the fifty-acre farm was purchased by Burgess Cochran ★

For the next fifty years, Cochran owned and nurtured the prosperous farm. He operated a dairy business on the property, raising a large herd of Jersey cows. He also had beef cattle and grew grain and vegetables. In the 1970s, the Bush family began to work for Cochran, helping him farm the land. Kenneth Bush remembers stacking and baling hay on the farm ★

Bush also recalls that Cochran was very proud of his produce, selling much of it at his roadside stand. He carefully tended his prize-winning cantaloupes, which were reputed to be the best around. Neighborhood children, knowing how fond he was of them, often crept into the garden at night to steal them ★

Cochran decided the best way to protect the plump melons was to put them under surveillance 'round the clock. Each evening, he crawled into his old Studebaker parked near the garden. Armed with his shotgun, he prepared to guard them for the night. And predictably, each evening, he fell asleep. The ritual only enhanced the children's midnight raids, and they created a ritual of their own. After securing their bounty, they each grabbed a handful of dirt and threw it against the car, so Cochran would know they had, once again, outsmarted him ★

In 1992, the Bush family bought their ancestor's farm. The family has extensive holdings in the area; their farms include 5,500 acres of grain. Their immense storage facilities tower over the flat fields and can be seen from Laban Brown's old barn ★

It is unlikely that Brown ever gave thought to what life would be like 150 years in the future. If he returned to the area, he would recognize his old barn and probably be surprised it is still standing. In his day, so many were lost to fire after being struck by lightening or catching a spark from machinery ★

The Bush family, Laban Brown's descendants, hopes he would be proud to have his barn represent the county he lived in for so many years. Harold, Kenneth, and Elizabeth Bush are pleased to own the Morrow County Bicentennial Barn ★

Muskingum

Owner
Jim and Violet Madden

Location
5040 Adamsville Road, in Zanesville

In 1799, the small town of Westbourn was established on the east bank of the Muskingum River. It was laid out by Jonathan Zane and John McIntire, who were gifted with the deed to the property by Zane's brother, Ebenezer. When the city was granted its first official post office, the settlement's name was changed to Zanesville. It became the county seat when Muskingum County was created in 1804. Surrounded by acres of farmland and framed with a picturesque white fence, Muskingum County's Bicentennial Barn is located on the Madden farm, a few miles northeast of the city ★

The history of the farm can be traced to January 9, 1832, when John Hague purchased 160 acres of land from the State of Ohio. Four years later, he sold it to Alexander Miller, credited with building the house, which still stands on the property. The first record of collected taxes was in 1838. At that time, the acreage was valued at $460 and the house at $240. Miller sold the farm to Henry Wheeler in 1862. Wheeler kept it for only a year before selling it to Sam O'Neal ★

O'Neal was an attorney and practiced law in his office on the farm. On a summer day in 1900, he prepared to leave town for a business trip. His farmhands, in the process of threshing wheat, were left working in the barn. The threshing machine caught on fire and took the barn with it. One of the workers saddled his horse and raced to the railroad station in nearby Dresden, hoping to find O'Neal before he departed. O'Neal shrugged off the news and continued with his planned journey, but quickly made arrangements to rebuild the barn. In the summer of 2000, when Scott Hagan painted the logo, the barn was exactly one hundred years old ★

O'Neal maintained ownership of the farm until 1923, when he sold it to Lemert Ferrell. By 1954, both house and barn had fallen into disrepair. Jim and Violet Madden purchased the property knowing it would be an ambitious task to restore the farm. They added a long, sloping shed to the barn,  replaced the roof, and made numerous repairs. The old farmhouse, expanded by several additions, was updated with modern conveniences ★

Today the farm, reduced to 134 acres, is an attractive composition of tidy outbuildings, quaint farmhouse, and sturdy white, bank barn. Madden uses the well-maintained barn to store hay and provide shelter for his herd of cattle. Jim and Violet Madden typify the hard working farmers who first settled in Ohio 200 years ago and have continued their agricultural traditions. They respect the history of their farm and are proud to own the Muskingum County Bicentennial Barn ★

Noble

OWNER
Kay Perkins

LOCATION
54043 Buffalo Township Road 110, in Pleasant City

Chosen to represent Noble County, Kay Perkins' little barn proudly displays the Bicentennial logo. Perched on a hillside, it welcomes visitors who pass through the county on Interstate 77. If the barn could speak, it might express surprise at the attention received since becoming a Bicentennial Barn. Once largely ignored by motorists on the highway, many now pull off the heavily-traveled road to photograph it. The more adventurous navigate the county's back roads to get a closer view ★

Kay Perkins purchased the farm in May of 2000. John and Julie Moore owned the farm for twenty-eight years, beginning in 1971. For many years, they raised cattle and tended huge gardens of vegetables. John Moore Jr., who now owns Moore Brothers Hardware in Byesville, remembers that his mother canned everything they grew ★

The barn was built in 1929, if the date carved on a huge beam is any indication. It still has the old hay hook, and the timbers are joined with mortise and tenon construction, held in place with square-head pegs. It was once an important part of the Drake Farm ★

Kay Perkins is proud to be a part of Ohio's Bicentennial celebration. Although the barn is used only for storage and an occasional Halloween party, she has no plans to tear it down. The barn will continue to stand, to greet travelers as they drive through Noble County ★

Ottawa

OWNER
Jim and Brenda Lowe

LOCATION
15794 W State Route 2,
in Oak Harbor

Jim Lowe grew up on this farm, where the windswept land is so flat you can see for miles in every direction. His great-great-grandfather bought the property in 1930. Included in the purchase were a farmhouse, built in 1890, and a large barn of approximately the same era. Lost to fire a few years later, the barn was replaced by a new one, which was built on the old foundation. Completed in 1936, it has sheltered livestock, protected grain, and withstood the violent storms that swept across the fields. Impeccably maintained, the barn stands ready and proud to represent Ottawa County ★

Construction of the Lowe barn circa 1936. Courtesy of Brenda and Jim Lowe.

It is a spacious barn, with a surface measurement of 8,000 square feet. From the ground to the peak of the roof, it stands forty feet high; add another six feet to reach the top of the cupola. The east end is actually a six-foot-wide corncrib, running the entire length of the barn ★

The Lowe farm has raised vegetables, grain, and livestock for as long as Jim can remember. When the farm operated at peak production, the barn was full to capacity with thirty to forty hogs and close to seventy head of beef cattle. Jim currently raises only a few of each ★

At the time the barn was constructed, a bucket elevator was installed to move grain throughout the barn. An auger in the floor carries the grain to one end of the barn and deposits it in a five-foot square pit. A huge chain, operated by gears in both the bottom of the pit and in the cupola, draws buckets of grain to a central location where chutes can direct it as needed. The device works off a twenty-amp, ten-horsepower motor and the transmission from a Model T car. The elevator is still in the barn and was in constant use until about ten years ago ★

The dedication ceremony brought at least 120 people to the tidy farm complex. Jim, who owns a catering business, set up a tent and arranged for food and beverages. After watching visitors try to photograph the barn around his field of corn, Jim planted wheat for the 2003 growing season ★

Jim and Brenda Lowe still live in the 1890s farmhouse. The placement of the house, barn, and outbuildings still gives the impression of a courtyard, an arrangement that has been followed by barn builders for years. The Lowes can sit on their back steps and look across the yard at the barn; it's a scene little changed since Jim's youth ★

The Lowes are proud and pleased to have their barn chosen to represent their county. Close to the Lake Erie Islands, there are many activities in the area to attract vacationers. Jim and Brenda Lowe anticipate the number of visitors to surge during the Bicentennial year, and they are ready to welcome them to their Ottawa County barn ★

Paulding

OWNER
Jim and Renee Carr

LOCATION
6227 US Route 24, east of Antwerp

Paulding County was one of the last areas in the state to be settled. The entire county, formed in 1820, was within the territory once known as the Black Swamp. By 1840, the population was only 1,025, the lowest of any county in Ohio. The process of draining the soil began in the 1870s, when engineers were hired to lay out 5,000 miles of ditches. Once completed, the drained land resulted in fertile farmland. According to a Department of Agriculture soil survey completed in 1991, there were 780 farms in Paulding County, covering close to eighty-six percent of the land ★

The barn selected to represent Paulding County can be found on one of those farms, a few miles east of Antwerp. Owned by Jim and Renee Carr, the thirty-six-acre farm has been in their family since 1949. Jim's parents, Wendell and Betty Carr, purchased 132 acres of farmland from Homer Smith. For ten years the property was share cropped, but when the tenant no longer wished to farm the land, Wendell and Betty moved their family onto the farm ★

The Carrs grew beans, corn, wheat, and oats on the land and raised approximately seventy head of dairy cattle. The barn, built in the mid-1930s, represents years of hard work and sweat equity to Jim Carr. When the family moved to the farm, Jim was already too old to enjoy playing in the barn. His older brother and sister soon left school and moved on, but Jim remained to help his father with the multitude of chores ★

In 1973, Wendell Carr passed away, and Jim took over management of the farm. He and his wife, Renee, moved into his parents' home, built between 1905 and 1906, and raised their daughter Betsy there. Betsy will graduate high school in 2003. She will celebrate her achievements as Ohio celebrates its 200th birthday ★

In June of 2000, the Bicentennial logo was painted on the Carrs' barn. Since then, the Carr family has acquired business interests in another area and has not been able to fully enjoy the experience of owning a Bicentennial Barn. The farm is presently for sale, giving someone else the opportunity to own a piece of Paulding County's history ★

Perry

OWNER
Ralph and Mary Catherine Holland

LOCATION
3783 US Route 22 NW, in Somerset

Perry County was formed in 1803, settled by Germans who emigrated from Pennsylvania. The county seat was first established at Somerset, the boyhood home of Union General Philip Sheridan. Sheridan was a superior horseman, his riding skills perfected in the hills and valleys around Somerset. A self-nominated candidate, he was accepted at the United States Military Academy in 1848 ★

In 1850, two years after he left Perry County, another of Somerset's citizens built a barn in one of those little valleys west of town. A few years later, he built a brick house high on a hillside overlooking the barn and his fields. For many years, the barn was alive with the sounds and smells of the farm. Today, although empty of livestock, it stands proudly as the Perry County Bicentennial Barn ★

In the mid-1900s, the 200-acre farm was owned by Charles and Nellie Emmert Reichley. With eleven children, the house was fairly bursting with activity, and there was no shortage of farmhands. As sons and daughters grew up and married, the close-knit family enveloped the spouses with love and acceptance. Mary Catherine Reichley Holland, who married son Dominic, enjoyed being a part of such a large family and looked forward to events on the farm ★

After Nellie's death, in the early 1970s, Mary Catherine and Dominic were able to purchase the farm. Dominic worked a full-time job during the day and returned at night to chores in the barn. Together, they raised a herd of beef cattle and worked for hours feeding them and tending to numerous tasks. Mary Catherine still remembers the sounds of the cattle as they chewed away on their feed. The barn was partitioned, and even the bull had a little feeding area of his own. As the cattle worked through their feed, Mary Catherine and Dominic spent time working, talking, and watching the ever-present barn cats ★

Dominic passed away in 1991, shortly after the couple celebrated their 25th wedding anniversary. With the help of his family, Mary Catherine continued to maintain the farm. Each morning she looked forward to the arrival of a nephew who would share a cup of coffee with her before beginning the day's necessary chores. But life changes. A few years later, Mary Catherine met Ralph Holland, also widowed, and the couple married ★

Today, the farm looks quite different. Numerous outbuildings that once cluttered the landscape were removed, including chicken coops and a garage. A shed was added to the barn, and the silo dismantled and removed by a group of Amishmen. The Hollands no longer raise cattle, and one of the Reichley nephews farms ninety-plus acres with corn and beans ★

Mary Catherine saw an article about the Bicentennial Barns and could hardly wait to mail in her application. When she learned her barn was selected, Mary Catherine was truly overjoyed. She and Ralph frantically repaired bits of siding, replaced a window here and there, and spent hours sweeping out the interior of the barn. Soon Scott Hagan arrived, threw up his scaffolding, and began to paint. Before he finished, the weathered barn had absorbed twenty-five gallons of paint ★

The local historical society contributed patriotic bunting and streamers, which they draped from beam to beam. Finally it was time for the dedication. The Reichley family stood proudly by as the barn on their old homestead officially became the Perry County Bicentennial Barn. Mary Catherine and Ralph are proud to own the barn and hope that when people view it they will think about Ohio's early farmers. Barns are the heart of the farm and a symbol of the hard-working families who settled in Ohio 200 years ago ★

Pickaway

OWNER
Mary Ann DeLong and Barbara Meade

LOCATION
5658 US Route 22, west of Circleville

In October, as nature paints the Ohio landscape with autumnal colors, farmers in Pickaway County deliver truckloads of pumpkins to the city of Circleville. Parades and pie-eating contests punctuate the annual Pumpkin Show. Originating in 1903, the show promotes the agricultural triumphs of Circleville and Pickaway County. Chosen to commemorate those triumphs is Pickaway County's Bicentennial Barn, owned by sisters Mary Ann DeLong and Barbara Meade ★

In 1900, just three years before the mayor of Circleville staged the first pumpkin display, Andrew Hoffman purchased a farm a few miles west of the city. It was familiar territory to him; he had lived on the property many years before, renting it from the previous owner ★

Andrew and his wife, Ella, raised their five children in a large farmhouse on the 391-acre farm. After his death in 1922, Ella moved into a smaller home in the city, leaving her sons to look after the farm. Son William took over after his marriage to Elizabeth, and together they raised another generation of Hoffmans in the family homestead ★

William Hoffman Jr. was born in the house and lived there until he was sixteen. Although the age of the barn has not been established, he can't remember a time when it wasn't there. He has memories of playing in the hayloft and crawling up into the cupola to catch pigeons. His father kept between twelve and fifteen horses in the barn and added several granaries for the storage of wheat. Farming in those days required many extra hands;

some lived in the tenant house on the property. In 1919, Andrew Hoffman built a concrete block building as housing for the migrant workers who came from Kentucky to help with the harvest ★

Hoffman barn. Courtesy of Pickaway County Historical Society.

The Hoffman family operated the farm until the death of Ella Hoffman in 1947. To settle her estate, William Sr. and his siblings sold the farm in September of 1948 to brothers William and Harold Defenbaugh. They hired Frank Mace, a recent veteran of World War II, to help them on the property. Frank stayed on for the next thirty-five years as farmhand and handyman ★

The Defenbaughs made several changes to the property. One of their first tasks was to tear off the rear part of the house, which may have been an addition to the original. The home was still quite large and housed Bill Defenbaugh's family after Harold's death. A silo was added to the barn, and the outbuildings were removed, including the concrete block building. The farm is presently owned by two of Bill's daughters, MaryAnn and Barbara. A family member lives in the old farmhouse, maintains the property, and looks after the barn. The barn has been well preserved, with tongue and groove siding and the original slate roof ★

The sisters are pleased their barn was chosen to represent the county and remain surprised by the publicity and public interest the project continues to generate. Since the dedication, the barn has been landscaped and tended by the Pickaway County Master Gardeners, who made the commitment to provide and maintain the flowers for ten years, changing the theme each spring. MaryAnn DeLong and Barbara Meade, along with their families, are delighted to own Pickaway County's Bicentennial Barn ★

Pike

OWNER
Keith and Sally Willson

LOCATION
*Intersection of State Routes 104
and 32, in Jaspar*

Jaspar was once a tiny village built on the banks of the Scioto River. Today, it is overwhelmed by the intersection of two main highways and the resulting traffic. Quaint buildings still stand as a reminder of its earlier days. There are several century homes, a tiny gas station that long ago stopped pumping gas, and a post office housed in a trailer. Sitting proudly on the northeast corner is the smallest of the Bicentennial Barns. So small, in fact, that the logo starts on the front and wraps around to finish on the side ★

The little barn is actually a corn-crib, built high off the ground and with adjustable slats on the sides to allow for maximum airflow. Although it is small in stature, one must not overlook its importance to history. Owner Keith Willson wishes the barn could talk to him and relay all the historic events it has witnessed ★

Built before 1850, the barn silently watched activity on the towpath of the Ohio and Erie Canal, constructed just a few hundred feet away. It survived the Civil War and a visit by Morgan's Raiders, one of whom killed a local man for refusing to row him across the river. In 1913, the building withstood the severe storms and flooding of the Scioto River. Years later, the barn saw the dirt roads on either side of it being paved and eventually becoming major highways ★

Keith and Sally Willson acquired the property from Robert Vulgamore in 1972. The purchase included the barn, a small house next to it where Sally's aunt now lives, and a pre-1850 house the Willsons call home. Behind the house is what, at first glance, appears to be a ditch. Closer inspection reveals huge blocks of stone cut and placed in position to form the sides of the Erie Canal. The Willsons discovered their house had been a coaching inn used by those who traveled on the waterway in its heyday. Keith often thinks about the teams of horses that must have driven along right behind his house and the constant activity in a village now overlooked by passing motorists ★

While some spend their vacations at the beach or on a cruise, the Willsons visit historic sites. It therefore seems appropriate that they would own this property. When their daughters were young, there were horses in the barn, but now it is used strictly for storage. They are committed to preserving it even though the recent widening of State Route 32 threatened its existence. The Willsons are pleased to have their barn chosen to represent Pike County and welcome all who stop by to see it ★

Portage

OWNER
Thomas and Christine Pfile

LOCATION
6205 Tallmadge Road, in Rootstown

In 1863, as the Civil War divided the country and tore apart families, William J. Payne invested in the future. On April 3 of that year, he purchased a forty-acre farm, south of Ravenna, in a small village called Rootstown. The farm has remained in the family for all but nineteen years and now belongs to Payne's great-great-grandson and his wife. Still standing on the farm is a barn Payne would recognize as his own. Owned by Thomas and Christine Pfile, the gray barn, with the distinctive red star on the gable, is Portage County's Bicentennial Barn ★

John Stearns first purchased the property, once part of the Western Reserve, from the State of Connecticut on September 11, 1815. Ten years later, on August 15, 1825, he sold it to Miner and D. Strong. When Payne bought the farm from Strong, he built a house and barn on the property. Two subsequent generations maintained the farm, but it slipped away from the family in the 1920s. At the height of World War II, on February 19, 1944, Harold and Dorothy Pfile bought back the family homestead ★

The Pfiles raised their children, Thomas and two sisters, on the farm. For many years, the pasture surrounding the barn was filled with dairy cows. As dairy farming became less profitable, the Pfiles changed to beef cattle. Thomas has many memories of growing up in the country, including the time he and his sisters became accidentally locked in the milk house, giving their parents quite a fright ★

The farm was broken up when Interstate 76 cut through the middle of the property in 1963. Harold then turned his attention to modifying the barn for a more practical use. Harold turned it into a garage by removing the cow stanchions, installing a false ceiling, and siding over the numerous windows. The oldest part of the barn still displays the logs used for framing, while a newer section has sawn timbers ★

Thomas and Christine purchased the property from Harold's estate on November 11, 1995. They continue to use the barn as a garage and for storage. The old farmhouse has been renovated but retains the charm of earlier days. Dorothy Pfile was in Eastern Stars and had a red star pieced into the linoleum floor of her kitchen. The flooring was recently replaced, but Christine didn't forget about the star. She asked Scott Hagan to paint a red star on the gable of the barn to honor Dorothy's memory ★

As they look out the window of their cheerfully remodeled kitchen, Tom points to a large tree, remembering a swing attached to a low branch now removed. Although Tom and his sisters used the swing from time to time, Penny Pfile, the family dog, got the most enjoyment from it. Penny, a boxer, was a gift to Harold, and he loved her. Providing amusement for the family, she would run out in the yard, grab the rope, and swing back and forth until it stopped. Then, perhaps hoping it would start up by itself, she would hang on with her teeth and simply wait. Motorists would stop, thinking the poor dog was dead and would approach the house to inform the owners. The dog, of course, would immediately let go of the rope and drop to the ground, causing the confused humans to shake their heads and walk away ★

Thomas and Christine feel honored to be chosen to help Portage County celebrate the Bicentennial. Thomas knows how much the farm meant to his father. Harold was born in the house, lived there most of his days, and died there. It was his life; a life he chose when he brought the farm back into the family. He would be proud to know his former dairy barn is standing as a symbol of Ohio's agricultural past ★

Preble

OWNER
Stephen Pope

LOCATION
*7903 US Route 127N,
in Lewisburg*

Dorothy and Carl Gauch were in their nineties when their 150-year-old barn was painted as the Preble County Bicentennial Barn. Outgoing and friendly, the couple was thrilled with the large crowd that assembled for the formal dedication ★

Among those who attended the celebration was Dorothy White, whose grandparents once lived on the farm. Dorothy was a little girl when a tragic farming accident claimed her grandfather's life. She carries the memory of being sent to pick up debris in the field where the accident occurred. Her grandfather's last name, Everding, is carved into one of the massive beams in the barn ★

Dorothy and Carl Gauch were interested in history and genealogy. They traced the path of the Gauch family as they emigrated from Germany and recorded the name of the ship's captain who brought them to the United States. The family settled in Preble County in the 1830s, and their descendents remained in the area ★

Dorothy and Carl purchased the 160-acre farm in 1958. It included an old farmhouse, a large dairy barn, a smaller tobacco barn, and several outbuildings. Located about a mile north of US Highway 40, the previous owners set aside a portion of their property for a small campsite. In the 1920s and 1930s, travelers on the National Road, as Highway 40 was called, frequently stopped to spend the night ★

The Gauches kept a herd of dairy cows, which were fed and sheltered in the barn and milked in the adjoining milking parlor. They operated the dairy there for several years but eventually sold the cattle and acquired sheep and ponies ★

Expanding on the idea of the original, little camping area, Dorothy and Carl ran a large campground on their farm from the 1960s through the 1980s. They loved people and enjoyed the social aspect of the business. The little tobacco barn was turned into an entertainment center for their guests. As they grew older, the work became too much for them to handle, and the campground was closed ★

In the late 1990s, Stephen Pope moved to the farm to live with Dorothy and his great uncle, Carl. Stephen had always been very close to the couple and savored the time he was able to spend with them. He was there to help around the house, and they appreciated the company ★

It was Stephen's idea to submit the barn for the painting project. He correctly guessed that the couple would be excited if chosen. Carl Gauch considered it nothing less than an honor to have his barn represent the county. Stephen is glad the dedication brought them so much pleasure, albeit for a short time. Both Carl and Dorothy died less than a year after the barn was painted ★

Although only seventeen acres remain of the original farm, Stephen wanted to keep it in the family. He feels fortunate that he was able to buy it from the estate. Furniture and other large items from the house and barn were sold at auction, but Stephen kept many personal items. He treasures his collection of old photographs, and smiles wistfully at an image of his diminutive aunt and uncle ★

Stephen's future plans include a long overdue renovation of the farmhouse. He fully intends to preserve and maintain the other buildings on the property. Although he has three sons he can recruit to help him, it is unlikely he will ever run out of projects. By purchasing the farm, Stephen is preserving the history of the Gauch family in Preble County. He is also keeping alive his own fond memories of a past generation. Dorothy and Carl would be proud ★

Putnam

Owner
James Kidd

Location
18716 State Route 65, in Columbus Grove

For $1,000 James Kidd could have had his barn torn down and hauled away. It was too old. It was too high. It was too costly to maintain. A metal shed or pole barn would have been more useful. But no price tag can be put on memories, and you never know when they are going to surface. James Kidd found that out before it was too late, and now he wouldn't consider tearing down the barn. Not even if someone paid him ★

James Kidd grew up on a farm about a mile and a half away from his present home. His father, Russell Kidd, raised cattle and chickens and grew wheat. In addition to farming his own land, he worked on a neighboring farm. The barn on the farm had been built with lumber milled at a nearby sawmill and was one of the first projects they did in the area ★

In 1939, Russell purchased the other farm. He acquired fifty-seven acres of land, an old farmhouse, and the barn. The previous owners had allowed a Mail Pouch Tobacco sign to be painted on the side. Russell, who was against smoking, could hardly wait to paint over it. Together, Russell and James worked on their farm, caring for the livestock, and harvesting the crops. It could have gone on like that for years, but World War II intervened. Russell Kidd lived long enough to see his son return from overseas, but passed away soon after ★

In 1955, James moved onto the property, by then reduced to forty-seven acres. For several years, he farmed the land as his father had done. Eventually, James gave up farming, and used the barn to store his tractors and miscellaneous items ★

In time, he began to think of the barn as a liability. As with many barns, it was built close to the road to facilitate bringing in a loaded hay wagon from the fields. It was then a simple matter to turn the wagon around in the road and back it up the ramp into the barn for unloading to the mow. But times changed ★

The road, that in his youth saw barely twenty-five cars a day, is now widened and paved, producing a constant rumble from traffic. Shortly before the Bicentennial Barn-painting project was announced, James decided it was time for the barn to go. He found someone willing to dismantle it for what he considered a reasonable price. He was ready, but fate intervened. Ohio was looking for a barn to represent Putnam County. Everyone told James they wanted it to be his barn. Someone from the local historical society sent in a photograph of the barn. A member of the Daughters of the American Revolution handed him a note in church, asking him to apply. James was amazed. In the end, he decided if that was what the community wanted, he wouldn't disappoint them. He painted the barn, did some basic repairs, and sent in the application. He soon received a letter notifying him he had been selected ★

As James prepared for the activities that would follow, he began to think about things he hadn't thought of in a long time. What the county was like when the barn was built and what events had taken place since. Memories, long suppressed, came flooding back. The barn had been there his entire life. He recalled how proud his father was on the day he finally purchased it. He remembered how hard his father had worked to make a living for himself and his family. He felt his father's pleasure at seeing his son serve his country and return alive. The barn was there throughout ★

When the barn was finally dedicated, an emotional James Kidd felt sure his father would have approved. James is determined to maintain it, and has vowed it will remain standing for as long as he lives. Area schools have brought children to the barn to study the history of Ohio. It will be up to their generation to preserve the barn and the tradition it represents ★

Richland

OWNER
Malabar Farm State Park

LOCATION
4050 Bromfield Road, in Lucas

After a decade of living in France, Pulitzer Prize-winning author, Louis Bromfield returned to the land of his birth before the outbreak of World War II. Bromfield had achieved success as a writer of both novels and screenplays for motion pictures. He had traveled around the world, and his list of friends included Hollywood stars, but he was homesick for the simple pleasures of his youth. Pleasures of life on a farm in Ohio. A native of Mansfield, he purchased four farms in nearby Lucas, an area once known as Pleasant Valley ★

Bromfield named his farm Malabar, after the Malabar Coast in India, the setting for one of his novels. It was a 640-acre collection of houses, barns, outbuildings, fields, and woods. A proponent of organic farming, long before it was fashionable, he saw the dangers of the use of chemicals and worked to improve soil and water resources. Malabar Farm became a State Park in 1976. Now over 900 acres, it contains many preserved buildings from the original four farms, including a barn known as the Richland County Bicentennial Barn ★

Once part of the Neiman estate, the barn was built in the 1800s. Bromfield used the barn for the storage of hay and grew produce on the acreage behind it. He built a roadside market across the street where he sold fresh vegetables to the public. The stand was popular with customers, not only for the quality of the product, but for Bromfield's celebrity guests, like Jimmy Cagney, who often sold produce. Today, the preserved market stand continues to sell organically grown, pesticide-free fruits and vegetables.

The market was constructed next to an elegant brick house, formerly the residence of David Schrack, his wife Elizabeth, and their fourteen children. The structure, built in 1820, faced Pleasant Valley Road, which became a heavily traveled stagecoach route. Schrack opened his large home to guests and eventually ran it as an inn. Bromfield used the spacious structure to house his many farm workers. The restored home is now the Malabar Inn, a restaurant serving home-cooked meals, using produce from the farm ★

With money derived from book royalties, Bromfield built a thirty-two-room house designed by himself and architect, Louis Lamoreux. The rambling farmhouse uses geothermal technology for heating, cooling, and humidification. The house was created to give Bromfield the space and solitude he needed for writing, spacious rooms for entertaining, and secluded bedrooms for his privacy-seeking guests. In 1945, it was the scene of Lauren Bacall and Humphrey Bogart's much-publicized wedding ★

Malabar Farm State Park is dedicated to preserving the memory and principles of Louis Bromfield. Visitors to the park can tour his house and see the farm as it was during his lifetime. Among the many buildings and sites to visit are a sugar camp, sawmill, smokehouse, corncrib, several barns, and the Bromfield cemetery ★

At Malabar Farm, Louis Bromfield found the tranquility he was looking for. He surrounded himself with all that he loved: his family, friends, books, music, acres of land, and his exuberant boxers ★

In his book, *Pleasant Valley*, he remembered to thank his ancestors for giving him a childhood in Ohio. The Richland County Bicentennial Barn pays tribute to Louis Bromfield and the many contributions he made to agriculture. Malabar Farm State Park continues his work, introducing a new generation of Ohioans to his ideals ★

Ross

OWNER
The Knoles Family

LOCATION
US Route 23, south of Chillicothe

The barn chosen to represent Ross County is located south of Chillicothe, on a farm owned by the Knoles Family. The road in front of the property is a heavily traveled, divided highway. Since the Bicentennial Barn was painted, motorists slow down and often pull off the road to look more closely. The large herd of deer that settles each night on the lawn by the barn, remains unperturbed by traffic and visitors. The Knoles family has only owned the barn for a few years, but their connection to it goes back much further ★

Charles (Buzz) Knoles was a teenager in the 1940s. After school, he would hop on his bike and ride into Chillicothe where he had a job working in his Uncle Johnny's store. Owned by his great-uncle, Johnny Mauger, it was an old-time, checker-playing general store, complete with pickle and cracker barrels and beans in big containers. In the summer months, Buzz helped Johnny on his farm. His most vivid memory is of standing in the haymow of the barn, right beneath the hot metal roof. It was his job to trample down the hay that flew along the rail and was dropped by the hayfork ★

The memories of those long, hot summer days stayed with Buzz. He was always fond of the land and remembered a little hay field with a valley. Even in his youth, he thought it would be a good place to have a lake. Years later, he returned to Chillicothe to settle down with his wife, Marlene. He recalled the hay field and approached his uncle about buying it. Johnny had no intention of selling any of his property but in time agreed to sell the parcel. Buzz and Marlene acquired the hay field and created the lake he always wanted ★

Eventually, the rest of the farm was sold and the property divided. In the 1970s, a family converted the barn into a craft shop called the Big Nail Barn. When the shop closed, the barn and house sat neglected for many years. At some point, the property was bought by a group of attorneys who rented it out ★

It occurred to Buzz that in the future it might be sold to someone who would build on it. As the land adjoined his property, he notified the attorneys that he would like to purchase it should they decide to sell. A few years later they contacted him, and in the early 1990s, Buzz Knoles bought back what was left of Uncle Johnny's farm ★

His first thought was to bulldoze the eyesore that used to be the farmhouse. Not only was the house neglected, but previous residents had kept livestock in it. The barn was another matter. Barely visible, it was completely overgrown with vines. Buzz and his son, Brian, hacked away at them with a chainsaw  to reveal the weathered siding. They had been told of a fire in the barn, so they entered it with caution. What they saw amazed them. Built in the 1930s, the barn was in surprisingly good condition, and there was no evidence of fire. Entirely constructed of oak, it was structurally sound. The rail and hayfork of Buzz's youth were still in place ★

Brian Knoles decided that he wanted to try to live on the property. After much deliberation, he totally remodeled the house. Then he went to work on the barn. Using rough-sawn timber from their property, Brian and

Buzz replaced pieces of rotted siding. The ground floor of the barn is now a workshop and recreation area. The upstairs has been left in its original condition ★

Brian is pleased when people who grew up in the area stop by to thank him for restoring it. A landmark of their youth, they remember when it was a working farm, and horses and slow-moving automobiles passed on the road in front of it. The barn is no longer used for its intended purpose; it is unlikely that it will ever again store hay, but the Knoles family is determined to preserve it for future generations to admire. They are proud to welcome you to the Ross County Bicentennial Barn ★

Sandusky

Owner
Sandusky County Agricultural Society

Location
Sandusky County Fairgrounds, in Fremont

In 1870, as Ohio was recovering from the Civil War, the Sandusky County Agricultural Society purchased acreage for a fairgrounds in Fremont. A year later, the board of directors approved a site plan for the building of three structures, including the barn, all of which are still standing. The architect, J.C. Johnson, also designed the home of President Rutherford B. Hayes and the Fremont City Hall ★

Appraised by the Ohio Preservation Office of the Ohio Historical Society, the barn is listed on the Ohio State Registry of Historical Places. The structure is a striking example of Victorian craftsmanship, boasting clipped gables at both ends and elaborate, decorative Carpenter Gothic millwork in the eaves. The wooden floor is tongue and groove and has no support columns or walls ★

The barn has been moved several times within the fairgrounds. It was first used as an exhibitor hall and later a dining hall. Most recently, it displayed items of the Sandusky County Historical Society, the Kin Hunters, and the Sandusky County Parks District ★

In 1999, the Agricultural Society started a Save Our Barn project to raise money for desperately needed foundation repairs. The historic building had been moved sixty years earlier to what was supposed to be a temporary location. In time, the wooden beams supporting it deteriorated and the groundhogs constructed an elaborate system of tunnels beneath it ★

The most cost effective way to preserve the barn was to prepare a new foundation and move the barn once again. The Agricultural Society joined forces with the Sandusky County Convention and Visitors Bureau to promote public interest. They held an antique auction and sold T-shirts to raise the necessary funds. When they learned that a barn was needed to represent Sandusky County for the Bicentennial, there was no doubt that this had to be the barn ★

In September 2002, the barn, standing proudly on its new foundation and adorned with red, white, and blue bunting, became the official Sandusky County barn. It also has the distinction of being the last of the eighty-eight barns to be painted and the only barn to have the logo painted on the roof.  A gala event was held with invitations going out to all of the Bicentennial Barn owners who were treated to a chicken dinner by the Lindsey Fire Department. The Governor of Ohio, Bob Taft, was on hand to assist painter Scott Hagan as he applied the final brush strokes ★

Scioto

OWNER

Clotavis Spriegle

LOCATION

Intersection of State Routes 139 and 335, in Minford

There have been many stories of the community spirit brought about by the Bicentennial Barn-painting project. None are more amazing than the enthusiasm displayed by the residents of Scioto County. They came from all corners of the county, answering a call for volunteers to help prepare Clotavis Spriegle's barn for the big event. Over one hundred people arrived to help on that first morning. In two days time, the job was done ★

Spriegle's red, gambrel-roofed barn was chosen due to its visibility. Built high above the highway, it can be seen from the intersection of two main roads, as well as the nearby airport runway. The barn was constructed in 1920 by Louis Poole. A prosperous farmer and accomplished furniture builder, Poole ordered plans for the barn and a house from Frank Lloyd Wright. Long a fan of Wright, Poole insisted upon filling his new home with furniture designed by the architect ★

Louis Poole and his wife, Vernella, moved onto the property when their son, Forrest, was 16. Forrest grew up with the knowledge his ancestry could be traced to the early English settlers of our country. His family is directly descended from one of the three babies born on the Mayflower as it lay anchored in Plymouth Bay ★

Forrest lived on his father's farm until he married in 1927. As his own family grew, he brought them to the farm every Sunday for dinner with his parents. His daughter, Donna, remembers summer afternoons spent there with her brother. Arriving after church, the two children would go immediately to the garden, cut a watermelon from the vine, and eat it while sitting in the field. Donna has another memory of life on the farm, which is lost to children of today. She grew up in a time when farmers still used milk cans. As a child, she was impressed with the huge containers her grandfather dragged down the drive to the edge of the road ★

Louis and Nellie sold their farm, in the 1940s, to Doctor Hunt and his family. Clotavis Spriegle acquired the property from them in 1983. She built a smaller home for herself and began renting out the large farmhouse. She and her son, Dwayne, use the barn for storage and to provide shelter for their herd of cattle ★

Spriegle first heard about the barn-painting project on a local radio station. She liked the idea but decided it would be too much work, and far too costly, to make the necessary repairs to her barn. She knew which side they would want to paint, and it was the side that was most damaged by the weather. Nichola Moretti, the regional coordinator for the Bicentennial Commission, drove by and spotted the barn. She made repeated visits and telephone calls to Spriegle, who finally agreed to let her barn be painted. And that's when it all began ★

A member of the area's local Bicentennial Committee asked for donations and volunteers. A lumber company graciously delivered boards to repair siding, a home improvement company supplied paint, the cable company brought a bucket truck, and someone else came

East end of barn visible from flight path of nearby Greater Portsmouth Regional Airport.

by with an air-nailer. The president of the school board, who teaches carpentry at the vocational school, offered to oversee the repairs ★

When the work began, volunteers arrived by the carload. They brought hammers and paintbrushes and spent hours in the blazing sun. Although

Spriegle had grown up in the area, people she had never met came to work on her barn. When barn-painter Scott Hagan commenced his part of the project, the steady flow of visitors continued. They brought coolers, set up lawn chairs, and monitored his progress ★

The dedication was a festive event. Food was provided by a collection taken earlier, and a soft drink company supplied beverages. Donna Poole Foehr returned to the county, from Michigan, to give a presentation about the history of the barn. Humbly grateful for the repairs to her barn, Clotavis Spriegle is still amazed at the way the community came together to support the project. The Spriegle Bicentennial Barn truly represents the farming traditions of rural Scioto County ★

Seneca

OWNER
Alberta and Larry Babione

LOCATION
7595 State Route 12, northeast of Fostoria

Seneca County was organized in 1824 and named for the Indian tribe that had a reservation within its boundaries. The land was flat and swampy, and the roads were poor. In 1851, work began on a toll road made entirely of wood planks. Known as the Plank Road, it connected the towns of Fostoria and Fremont. The heavily-traveled road passed through a large tract of land owned by the Stockwell family ★

Railroads soon became the preferred method of transporting goods, and use of the road declined. The road, now known as State Route 12, bisects the farm owned by Alberta and Larry Babione. Recent work by state road workers revealed remnants of wood from the deteriorating planks ★

The Babiones have lived on the property since 1982. They purchased four acres, including a house and barn, from Don Hanover of Hanover Farms. The big, white farmhouse was over a hundred years old. Used by Hanover as rental property, it needed to be updated. After extensive remodeling, the Babiones filled it with their collection of antiques and decorative items, many created by Larry ★

The barn is thought to be about seventy-five years old. Alberta, who grew up on a farm in the area, remembers hearing that the original barn burned down. No changes have been made to the barn; the old stalls and haymow are still there. Currently, the barn is used for storage of Larry's antique tractors, a 1939 Ford N and a 1939 Allis Chalmers B ★

Civil War reenactors, from Gilmor's Battery, assembled for the dedication of the barn. To add a touch of nostalgia, they brought a canon from Spiegel Grove in Fremont. With careful timing, the canon was fired just as the ribbon was cut. Unpredicted, the resulting thick, black smoke, temporarily obscured the ceremony from view, providing a note of humor ★

Larry and Alberta are proud their barn was selected and enjoy sharing it with their six children and nine grandchildren. They continue to maintain the property for the enjoyment of everyone who stops to see it. Much to their delight, busloads of area schoolchildren have been brought to have their class photos taken in front of the barn ★

Larry is especially proud of the way the barn looks at night, lit in a red, white, and blue theme. The illuminated Seneca County Bicentennial Barn shines like a beacon on the otherwise dark, country road and can be seen for a good distance traveling east from Fostoria on the old Plank Road ★

Shelby

OWNER
Greg and Rita Schwer

LOCATION
2540 West Mason Road, in Sidney

Barns across Ohio are lost every year to fire, demolition, and neglect. The cavernous structures are no longer practical for many farmers today, and the cost to restore is often prohibitive, regardless of the sentiment involved. Greg and Rita Schwer purchased their two-acre farm specifically because it had a barn. Now that is has become the Shelby County Bicentennial Barn, the Schwers are more determined than ever to preserve it for future generations to enjoy ★

The Schwers purchased their farm from Richard Ernst. Richard's grandparents, Henry and Mary Ernst, bought the property in 1922. Richard recalls hearing that Henry and Mary passed by the farm on their monthly shopping trips into Sidney. Henry admired the farm and often remarked that someday he would find a way to buy it. Richard doesn't know when the barn or house was built, but is sure both were there long before his grandfather purchased the farm ★

Henry and Mary transferred ownership to their children in the 1940s. Later, Richard acquired the property from his parents, also named Henry and Mary. For many years the farm was rental property. In 1974, the Ernst family tore down the old farmhouse and built a new home. They sold the house, barn, and two acres of their farm to the Schwers in July 1998 and continue to farm the remaining acreage ★

Rita Schwer loves her timber-frame barn. Built in the time-honored tradition of mortise and tenon joinery, it measures forty feet by seventy feet. When Greg and Rita acquired the barn, they considered several options for adaptive use. They thought about living in it but rejected that as too costly. Their three children, a boy and two girls, had other ideas. They wanted the barn to stay a barn ★

The Schwers' son began working for a hog farmer and saved his money to buy his first pig. For the next few years, the family was involved in raising hogs for 4-H. Not all of their son's friends were lucky enough to have a barn, and the Schwer barn had ample room for livestock. Rita and Greg invited them to use space in their barn. Rita watched as week after week her son and his friends learned how to build pens and care for the animals. It was a good experience, she feels, and gave them a sense of responsibility ★

Long before the Bicentennial logo was painted, the Schwer barn caused a sensation in the neighborhood. Rita, who has an artistic flair, designed and constructed a modern nativity. Adorned with small white lights, it was displayed on the end of the barn now occupied with the logo. People often commented that seeing it gave them a sense of peace and serenity, especially at night when it illuminated the barn and sent a glow across the wide field ★

Rita Schwer still has plans for her barn. Now that her children are growing up, she would like to turn the barn into a party center for weddings, showers, and receptions. She is looking for a way to finance the project, which she admits is still a few years away. For now, she and her family are content to own Shelby County's Bicentennial Barn. She extends a welcome to all who want to visit and has decided to return the nativity to the barn, but in a different location, so as not to interfere with the logo. She thinks the two symbols will coexist nicely. One pays homage to the grit and determination of our forefathers, the other confirms their faith ★

Stark

<small>OWNER</small>
Merle and Linda Tomlinson

<small>LOCATION</small>
State Route 172, between New Franklin and Paris

To increase public awareness of Ohio's 200th birthday celebration, the Ohio Bicentennial Commission produced a video titled *A Time to Celebrate*. The presentation chronicled Ohio's history and was punctuated by film footage of Scott Hagan painting the Bicentennial logo on the Stark County barn. Owned by Merle and Linda Tomlinson, the former dairy barn can be found in gently rolling countryside on State Route 172, between New Franklin and Paris ★

In 1869, Jim Miller carved his name and the year into a large piece of sandstone he found in the pasture. He is credited with building the dairy barn in 1875. His brother-in-law, whose last name was Wartman, became the next owner of the farm and built a house on the property in 1890. Once completed, he decided the structure was too nice to live in, and he moved into the summerhouse. He did, however, stipulate that his funeral be held in the house. Perhaps he had a portent of the future, for he died three years later ★

Fred and Pauline Tomlinson purchased the 150-acre farm in 1933 from the Baxter family. The farmhouse still had the black walnut staircase Wartman built and was topped with a cupola, which Fred promptly removed. Fred made no major changes to the barn but added a shed in 1942 ★

The Tomlinsons raised dairy cattle, a tradition their son, Merle, continued when he acquired the property in 1993. The farm is now 139 acres, and much of the land is leased. The restored farmhouse and two acres of property belong to the Tomlinsons' son. The barn, which used to be red, has been in continuous use. Heat produced by the cattle has helped to protect the barn from decay. It has been carefully maintained and has new siding and a new roof ★

The actual painting of the barn received more attention than expected. Members of the community turned out early to watch the proceedings and were quickly joined by curious motorists. It soon became so congested, law enforcement officials found it necessary to temporarily close the road. And it didn't stop there. The dedication went on into the evening, with ample amounts of food and a live band for entertainment. The event culminated with a red, white, and blue fireworks display, all captured on film. The image of the pyrotechnics was added to a limited edition miniature of the barn produced by Cat's Meow ★

The film crew is gone, and the smoke from the fireworks has long since dissipated. The Stark County barn continues to sit, as it has done for over a hundred years, nestled in a little valley surrounded by farmland. It remains stoic, as cattle mill about in the barnyard, just as they always have. For Merle Tomlinson, it is a window to his past, a reminder of his father and a tribute to hard-working dairy farmers throughout the state. Although he no longer lives on the farm, Merle is at home there. Farming is in his blood, as it was for so many of our ancestors, the pioneers who settled Ohio 200 years ago ★

Summit

OWNER
Adrienne Cole Chambers

LOCATION
3742 Hudson Drive, in Stow

Dora Mae Hawkins had happy memories of growing up in the 1930s and '40s. As a teenager, she often rode horses on a farm owned by the Davis Riding Academy in Stow. She was delighted, then, when her father, Sylvanius W. Hawkins, purchased the nineteen-acre farm in the mid-1940s ★

Although the property came with a barn, his dream was not to be a farmer but to start his own business. To accommodate the equipment he would have to acquire, Hawkins removed the horse stalls, added electricity, and cemented the lower level of the former horse barn. In 1947, Hawkins Machine opened its doors ★

The machine shop thrived, as did the vegetables in the huge garden he grew each year behind the barn. Located in a valley formed by the tributary of a nearby river, the land surrounding the barn was swampy but fertile. Hawkins referred to his property as Muck Farm ★

Sylvanius Hawkins ran his machine shop until 1961, when his son-in-law, Richard Cole, Dora Mae's husband, took over. Richard and Dora Cole had three daughters, two who graduated with degrees in interior design. In 1979, daughter Adrienne decided to leave the design business and work with her father to learn machining from the ground up. Her sister, the other design major, joined her, and the two girls assumed ownership of the business in 1997. They continued to operate the machines their grandfather had purchased pre-owned, during World War II. It is a family run machine shop dedicated to detail and accuracy and specializes in ring-dies construction ★

Except for Hawkins' modifications, the barn has remained in its original condition. Based on its size and construction, the barn appears to have been built in the early 1800s as an English, three-bay threshing barn. Later, it was altered to become a bank barn with windows on three sides of the lower level. In 1996, the barn was jacked up to stabilize the crumbling stone foundation. On the west side, which had buckled badly, the windows were removed, cement blocks were added, and new siding was installed. The barn is used for storage now, but the upper level is original. A team of horses could still be driven in and hay unloaded into the mow ★

Stow has changed dramatically since Hawkins opened his business. It is no longer a rural, farming community. The road in front of the barn, one of the first in the area, has been regraded and paved, and a new highway was constructed through the middle of the farm. Just down the street are fast food restaurants and large retail establishments. The barn seems out of place now, a symbol of what life used to be ★

The machine shop has seen its heyday, too. Business has fallen off in recent years, and soon Hawkins' granddaughters will have to make a decision about selling the business that was their grandfather's dream. They hope that a future caretaker will have his or her own dream and that it will include preserving the barn ★

Trumbull

OWNER
Jim Marsh

LOCATION
7763 E Liberty, in Hubbard

The Bicentennial Barn-painting project began as a way to involve the public in Ohio's 200th birthday celebration. Since its inception, it has drawn attention to all of Ohio's remaining barns, many crumbling and on the verge of collapse. Although some barn owners are ambivalent about their barns, most see them as a link with happier, more peaceful, days gone by. They are trying their best to preserve the great structures for another generation to appreciate. Nowhere is that spirit of preservation more evident than in the Trumbull County barn ★

Before the restoration! Courtesy of Jim Marsh.

In the 1800s, this farm was called the Indian Run Dairy. Owned by the Price family, it was a huge complex of several hundred acres, with a small creek running through the middle. In 1932, the dairy barn was destroyed by fire. No farm owner could do without a barn for very long, and the Price family commissioned architect Harry J. Beck, of Ashtabula, to draw up plans for a replacement ★

Upon completion of the new barn in 1935, the family business reopened as the Price Brothers' Dairy. Constructed as a bank barn, there was ample room for the dairy herd on the lower level, storage space for tractors and equipment on the next floor, and above, an expansive haymow. The barn had the added convenience of wide, sliding doors on all four sides ★

Dorothy Price was the last of the family to live on the farm. She sold much of the property, including one hundred adjoining acres, for the development of the Deer Creek Golf Course. Dorothy continued to live in the 1800s-era farmhouse, the Price family homestead. She worried about her continuing ability to maintain the property, but did not want the house and barn to be razed by a developer ★

Although the acreage was sought by many, Dorothy chose a buyer carefully. Enter, Jim Marsh. Jim was known in the area for his restoration of other historic properties in the county. Dorothy trusted him to carry out her vision, and in 1995, Jim Marsh bought the Price farm. His purchase included a house, barn, and several outbuildings. All needed extensive work ★

Dorothy Price must be pleased. The farm complex has been meticulously restored, including the silo and a little building that may have been a child's playhouse. Jim documented his progress on film, as the restoration project unfolded. He recently shared some of those photographs with school children who were learning about Ohio's history through the barn-painting project. Among his treasured memorabilia are milk bottles from the former dairy and the architect's blueprints for the barn ★

Jim is not a farmer, so he uses the barn only for storage of equipment and miscellaneous items. It is a tribute to his tenacity that the barn was chosen to represent Trumbull County. Had it not been for his preservation efforts, the barn might easily have been destroyed. He is pleased to present the former Price Brothers' Dairy for a new generation of Trumbull County residents to admire ★

Tuscarawas

OWNER
Vernon and Rachel Mutti

LOCATION
2960 Stone Creek Road SW, in Stone Creek

Tuscarawas County was named for the land's native inhabitants, the Tuscarawas Indians. The area's first permanent white settlers were of German and Swiss descent, and arrived in 1803. The Mutti barn was chosen to represent those early families as the Tuscarawas County Bicentennial Barn ★

Five generations of the Mutti family have lived in Stone Creek. Peter Mutti, from Switzerland, was the patriarch of the family. He was the first to settle on the 128-acre farm, in the mid-1800s. William and Catharine were the next to acquire the property, later purchased by their son Cletus. Another son, Emmett, bought his mother's homestead, located a few miles down the road ★

The barn and house on the farm were built in the early 1900s, probably by William Mutti. The property was used as a dairy farm until Cletus Mutti's death, in January of 1970. His wife, Eleanor, lived in the old farmhouse for a year, finally deciding to move out of the area ★

In the spring of 1971, Eleanor Mutti sold the farm to her nephew and his wife, Vernon and Rachel Mutti. Eventually, the house and three acres of property were sold, but they kept the barn and remaining acreage ★

The Mutti family continues the farming tradition started by Peter Mutti in the early years of the county. Today, the family owns the Mutti Dairy Farms. Partners in the business include Vernon and his two sons, Keith and Kevin. The Mutti family is proud to own the Tuscarawas County Bicentennial Barn ★

Union

OWNER
Bob and Donna Clady

LOCATION
24759 State Route 4, in Richwood

In 1840, a political party known as the Whigs announced that it would hold a convention in Columbus and invited all the Ohio counties to attend. Each county endeavored to take something to the convention that would be unique to their area. Many wrote songs to describe a virtue of their county. At that time, newspapers across the country had printed unflattering comments about Ohio's presidential candidate, William Henry Harrison. A Whig, he was ridiculed for living in a log cabin, although most people did at that time ★

Someone in Union County had the idea of building a cabin and transporting it to the convention. Using logs from a buckeye tree, they constructed the little building right on the wagon that would take it to Columbus. Otway Curry, of Marysville, even contributed a song he penned titled *Log Cabin Song* ★

The tune quickly became popular at the convention and soon spread from state to state. Harrison's ensuing campaign became known as the "Log Cabin Campaign," and Ohioans were forever referred to as Buckeyes. The Union County Bicentennial Barn, owned by the Clady family, sits on land formerly owned by one of those first Buckeyes ★

The property was originally deeded to Colonel William Langstaff, a Revolutionary War veteran, as payment for his services. By 1929, the farm was owned by Marcus Eblin, known to everyone as Pop. The first barn on the property was lost in a fire, and Pop determined he would build a new one over the old foundation. Timber for the frame was cut from hardwoods on his farm. To obtain milled wood for the siding, Pop made daily trips to Marion and returned with his team of horses pulling the load of wood ★

Lester and Margaret Eblin, Pop's son and daughter-in-law, were the next owners of the property. The couple used the barn for their livestock, both hogs and dairy cattle, and stored loose hay in the mow. The Depression made it necessary to change the way they did business. To make ends meet, Lester and Margaret raised chickens in the haymow and sold them to the Harding Hotel in Marion. They delivered feed and water to the mow by rigging a pulley system ★

Bob and Donna Clady lived with their families just down the road from the Eblins and referred to them as Uncle Lester and Aunt Margaret. The two children grew up, went to school together, and eventually married. In 1976, the Cladys purchased the Eblins' 187-acre farm and moved into the old farmhouse on the property. The oldest part of the house was built in 1859 and sits on four huge cornerstones. The foundation is composed of enormous logs from an old walnut grove. In the 1920s, an addition expanded the size of the house, and Bob and Donna enlarged it further by adding to the back in 1995 ★

Bambi

Few changes have been made to Pop Eblin's old barn. The siding is original, as is most of the standing-seam roof, although some of that was lost in a tornado. The Clady's grow corn, soybeans, wheat, and hay on their land and raise cattle. The barn shelters the family's beloved saddle horses. Bob and Donna have two daughters who grew up on the farm. When they were young, they played in the barn, as children with the opportunity seem to do. They set up their trampoline in the broad center bay and took turns leaping up to grab and swing on the old hay rope. Bob and Donna hope that one day the farm will belong to one or both of the girls ★

The Cladys knew nothing of the barn-painting project until the regional coordinator stopped at their farm and asked it they would like to have the Bicentennial logo on their barn. Much to the Cladys' surprise, their barn turned out to be the forty-forth barn painted, the halfway point of the project. Governor Taft was on hand for the dedication and added his paint strokes and signature to the barn ★

Bob and Donna own and operate Nature's Bounty, a garden center and greenhouse. They sell annuals, perennials, and statuary. There is also a small gift shop. The Clady family is delighted to own the Union County Bicentennial Barn and extend a warm welcome to visitors ★

Van Wert

OWNER
Betty and Lewis Linton

LOCATION
16115 Lincoln Highway, in Van Wert

The historic Lincoln Highway winds its way along a strip of land locals call "the ridge." At the end of the glacial period, this sandy ridge formed the shoreline of Lake Erie. It was a well-traveled Indian trail, and for many years, farmers found artifacts when they turned over their soil. To the north of the ridge lay the Black Swamp, where the land was level and the lake bed soil fertile. Years later, pioneers would travel and settle there, building homes and farms along the ridge ★

In 1937, it was decided the Lincoln Highway should be paved with concrete instead of gravel. To facilitate the process, the road was straightened and rerouted to the north, following the path of the ridge. That same year, when Roger Richie was ten years old, his father's landlord elected to build a new barn. He hired Bill Stemen, a well-known barn builder, to design and construct it. They decided to situate the barn facing the new Lincoln Highway. Richie recalls it was the highlight of his youth, having two such momentous events occur simultaneously in front of his house ★

In the early 1930s, the 178-acre farm belonged to John Marsh. The Depression got the best of many men, and John was one of them. He lost the farm when the bank foreclosed on his mortgage. In 1935, the barn on the property burned down, and Homer J. Gilliland, president of the local bank, purchased the acreage as an investment. He rented the house and land to Paul Richie and his family. They were living in the farmhouse on the property when Gilliland arranged for the new barn to be built ★

The barn was designed for use as a dairy barn. The shed, added to the rear of the barn, is sixteen by seventy feet. It was used as a milking parlor and cow stable. The main barn measures thirty-six feet wide by seventy feet long. To facilitate the storage of hay, the center section of the mow is open to the roof, requiring extensive support. Many barns were weakened by relentless wind and the pressure produced by a full mow of hay ★

Recognizing that the wind picks up speed as it crosses the ridge, Bill Stemen used supporting tie beams called swell bellies to handle the added stress. The boards, placed on each end of the mow, connect the purlins. Cut from one log, each board measures eight by eight inches at the ends and burgeons to twelve or sixteen inches in the middle ★

In 1967, Lewis and Betty Linton rented the farm from Russell Gilliland, Homer's son. Twenty years later, they purchased it from the Homer Gilliland Trust. Time had taken its toll on the buildings. The farmhouse had been torn down, along with a corncrib. Referred to as an Illinois crib, the little building was hip-roofed with a cupola for ventilation and possessed a horse-driven elevator ★

Lewis has made a few changes to the barn and only minimal, but necessary, repairs. He had a new roof installed, removed the horse stalls, and replaced the doors. At the time the barn was built, fourteen feet was the traditional width for barn doors. Lewis cut back the overhang above the horse mangers, and increased the door width to twenty feet ★

Lewis and Betty Linton are proud to own Van Wert County's Bicentennial Barn. Lewis even went so far as to plant wheat on either side of his barn for the 2003 growing season. He wanted the barn to look its best for visitors and photographers. The Lintons were so pleased with the painting of the logo, they hired painter Scott Hagan to return and paint the west end of the barn. They have chosen to have an American flag depicted, and the words "One Nation, Under God." The barn will stand as a tribute, not only to Ohio's farming tradition, but also to our country ★

Vinton

OWNER
Eugene and Garnet Engle

LOCATION
27754 State Route 93, in McArthur

The Engles' Bicentennial Barn was built before the Civil War. Originally part of the Johnston farm, it narrowly escaped a visit by Morgan's Raiders, and was visited by gypsies on their annual migration through the county. It is wistfully remembered as a perfect playground for children, a place to play inventive games, and test one's balance by walking the beams ★

In the early 1800s, a large log cabin was built on the property. It became an inn, a place for travelers to rest and water their horses. Thomas Johnston purchased the cabin and surrounding acreage, and in 1860, he constructed what is now the upper level of the barn. Perhaps deterred by the Civil War, he finished the project in 1865, creating a lower level built into the natural bank of the earth ★

In 1874, Thomas began to build a farmhouse opposite his barn and close to the road. The narrow road crossed the creek on the property by means of a small covered bridge. When the house was completed, the family moved in, and Thomas tore down the old log cabin. Two doors from the old structure were used on the second floor of the new house, where they remain today. His great-granddaughter, Alice Jane Greathouse Ellison, remembers her mother saying that the massive stone fireplace stood on the farm for many years ★

James Carney Johnston, Thomas' son, became the next owner of the property. He and his wife, Alta, raised their six children in the farmhouse, one of which was Mary, Alice Ellison's mother. Once a year, a band of gypsies stopped by the spring on the farm and camped for a few days. As they caused no harm, the Johnstons allowed them to stay. The children, however, were terrified of them and went to great lengths to avoid passing near them, often taking the long route through the woods on their way to and from school ★

Mary and one of her brothers walked to school in Creola. It was a long walk, especially in the harsh winter months, and James would pull out his little red sleigh, throw on the bells, and harness the horses. The children called it the Santa Claus Sleigh; it had the curved runners so often seen in artists' renderings of the chubby, red-suited, little man and his reindeer. James would drive the horses to the school and be there waiting to take them home. Years later, when the wagon shed was torn down, the family found the red sleigh, as well as the wagon Thomas used when he emigrated from Pennsylvania ★

The Johnstons were great storytellers. They collected tales and handed them down to the next generation. Mary Johnston loved to tell about her three brothers' escapade with their pony, Topsy. The three boys were ages three, four, and six. While Mary, who was five, watched with great interest, they brought Topsy into the house and up the stairs to the room they shared on the second floor. Topsy could do "up," but "down" was simply out of the question. James rigged up block and tackle and lifted the pony back to level ground ★

Mary Johnston married C.D. Greathouse and moved to McArthur. Greathouse worked for a gas and oil company and was often gone. When Mary was pregnant with Alice, he took her back to the Johnston farm so her family would be with her. That evening, Alice decided it was time to enter the world. She was the last child born at the Johnston homestead ★

Alice's uncle John took over management of the farm, and Alice and her siblings spent many enjoyable days on the farm. Alice, who admits she was a tomboy, loved playing in the barn with her brother, John, and a cousin Tommy, who was close in age. Whatever the two boys did, Alice did. That included walking on the barn's massive beams that towered high above the floor. Alice is proud to say that she never fell or broke any bones ★

In the 1940s, the road in front of their house was moved and upgraded. The little covered bridge that had enchanted them as children was demolished. The Johnston family sold the farm to Eugene and Garnet Engle in 1981. It was a heartbreaking day for the Johnstons, but no one was left who wanted the responsibility. The farm had changed, and their fairy-tale world had ended. Sadly they walked away ★

The Engles have made few changes to the farm. Irises, peonies, and chives still come up where they were first planted. Today, the farm is bordered by a tidy, white rail fence, and horses graze peacefully in the field. The farmhouse is restored for use as a guesthouse and for entertaining ★

Alice Jane Ellison and all of her remaining family are welcome to visit. They are assured they may spend the night if they become nostalgic about their farm. Eugene and Garnet Engle have become the caretakers of this historic property and are pleased their barn was chosen to represent Vinton County ★

Warren

OWNER
Tom and Brenda Neeley

LOCATION
6012 State Route 48, north of Lebanon

The Neeleys never expected to be on television, but that is what happened when their eighty-three-year-old barn became the Warren County Bicentennial Barn. Brenda Neeley first saw an article about the barn project in a magazine. Before she could submit her name, the Bicentennial regional coordinator saw the barn and decided it would be perfect. The Neeleys were easily convinced, and before they knew it, their barn was painted, and the camera crews had arrived ★

Brenda Neeley grew up on this property, in the hilly countryside on the outskirts of Lebanon. Her parents, Eileen and Floyd Smith, bought the sixty-acre farm in the 1930s. For years, friends and family called Eileen Smith by her nickname: Sugar. Brenda, being the only child and a daughter, was naturally called Little Sugar. Floyd, looking for a name for his property, hit upon the idea of calling it Sugar Hill Farm. The farm retains that name today, and visitors to the property drive under the canopy of towering sugar maples Floyd planted long ago ★

As a little girl, Brenda loved to play in the barn. She enjoyed being around the animals that were fed and sheltered there, including cattle, horses, and sheep. Often she would climb up to sit in the haymow. The sound of mewing meant that somewhere in the hay she would find a litter of tiny kittens ★

The smells of the barn were magnified on rainy days. Brenda has only to see a photograph or painting of sheep to recall the smell of their warm wool. It was common for their sheep to have twins, and the mother would invariably reject one of them. Brenda has fond memories of bringing the newborns into the house and drying them off with a hairdryer before returning them to the barn ★

In 1992, Brenda Neeley moved back to the farm with her husband, Tom, and their son, Russell. The farm is only twelve acres and there no longer are animals grazing in the fields. The barn is used as an oversized garage. The Neeleys park their cars and tractor inside, and also use the barn for storage of large items ★

Brenda hopes to make some improvements to the barn so Russell can begin using it for his 4-H projects. He enjoys sharing photographs of the Bicentennial Barn with classmates. It has been a learning experience for him to discover the part his family played in the history of Warren County. The Neeleys are pleased their barn was chosen as the representative barn for their county. Tom, Brenda, and Russell look forward to meeting many new people as Ohio prepares to celebrate its Bicentennial. They are proud to welcome visitors to Sugar Hill Farm ★

Washington

OWNER
Stephen and Mary Rachel Carr

LOCATION
State Route 60, in Lowell

In 1913, the waters of the Muskingum River extended their reach well beyond previous levels, demolishing most of the small towns that lined its banks. North of Marietta, the little community of Lowell was virtually destroyed. Residents sought shelter wherever they could find it, and that included moving in with the livestock. Thus, the Washington County Bicentennial Barn served, for a time, as a residence for its former owners. Presently owned by the Carrs, it is one of the few buildings to survive the flood. Today, the barn proudly welcomes visitors to historic Washington County, the first county formed in Ohio ★

The pioneer settlement in Lowell was established in April of 1795. Four cabins were built on the riverbank, surrounded by a fortification. After the Treaty of Greenville, the fear of Indian attacks diminished, and the early residents moved onto their own farms. Lowell slowly grew into a prosperous farming community. The 1913 flood caused destruction to homes and businesses, the Opera house, a bandstand, and bridges over the river. It was a blow the town never fully recovered from ★

Families wanted to begin construction of new homes at once, but building materials were not readily available. The mills were gone, torn apart just as their houses had been. As the floodwaters receded, the enterprising residents salvaged wood from the debris left behind. The attic of the Carrs' home displays boards of different sizes, and the rafters are still covered with mud from the saturated ground ★

The farm, now owned by Stephen and Mary Rachel Carr, was developed by the Wagner or Waggoner family. It is believed that they had the barn built in the late 1800s. The floor joists are made from logs flattened on two sides, and the timber framing is all hand-hewn. The upper level of the barn has plank flooring, installed when the barn was used as a home. The lower level of the bank barn, where the livestock was kept, has a dirt floor ★

During World War II, the Oliver family lived on the farm. They used the barn for their dairy cattle. The barn became a billboard, with a Mail Pouch Tobacco sign occupying one end and advertising for the local drugstore painted on the other ★

The Carrs purchased the thirty-two-and-a-half-acre farm in 1980. They grow hay and corn and raise cattle. The barn is used to store baled hay and farm equipment, both new and old. Stephen has a collection of 1940s and 1950s farm machinery, including a tractor from the 1940s, an Allis Chalmers B ★

Since owning the farm, the Carrs have renovated the farmhouse and made repairs to the barn, including a new roof. While working on the house, they found a letter concealed in a wall. Dated 1914, the writer expressed amazement at the new-fangled invention known as an automobile ★

Stephen and Mary Rachel Carr are proud to own the Washington County Bicentennial Barn. Marietta, site of the first Ohio settlement, will be the scene of many Bicentennial events in 2003. The Carrs are looking forward to the visitors who will stop to view their barn, and they extend a warm welcome from the little town of Lowell ★

Wayne

OWNER
Scot Industries

LOCATION
6500 Ashland Road, west of Wooster

The rural atmosphere of Wayne County is the perfect backdrop for one of the newest of the Bicentennial barns. The surrounding countryside is home to a large Amish population, whose horse drawn buggies are a common sight on the county's roads. Built in the 1940s, the Gothic-roof, three-end barn is owned by Scot Industries. It can be found on State Route 250, a curving, two-lane road running diagonally across the county through the college town of Wooster ★

The history of the farm can be traced to 1908, when P. C. Firestone bought the property, including a house, barn, and outbuildings, for his daughter and son-in-law, Bessie and Lloyd Thorley. In 1925, Bessie and her husband purchased the farm from Firestone, where they raised their only son, Omar. When he married, it was decided the old farmhouse was large enough to accommodate both families. Omar and his wife, Ruth, lived in the west end of the house, while Bessie and Lloyd lived in the east, closest to the barn ★

It was Bessie who saw it first. She awakened, on a winter night in 1944, to see the orange glow of a barn on fire. Their barn. The flames lit the February sky in all directions. A friend, who lived two miles away, got out of bed and could see to dress without the need for electricity. Everything in the barn was lost to the intense heat: thirty-six head of cattle, four horses, and a brand new tractor ★

Construction of straw shed circa 1961.
Courtesy of Eloise Thorley Snoddy.

The Thorleys needed a new barn at once, and so they hired builders Harvey and Ben Imhoff. The brothers were well known in the county for constructing Gothic-roof barns. By 1920, barns with round roofs had become a popular choice for farmers. In addition to its visual appeal, the framing technique provided a haymow without any obstructions. As the brothers began to work, neighbors stopped to donate trees from their farms as lumber for the new dairy barn ★

Eloise Thorley Snoddy grew up on the farm, as did her three sisters and brother. With so many people living there, life inside the house could be a little chaotic. For reasons Eloise can't remember, she and her siblings referred to both their mother and grandmother as Mom. As a child, it was not entirely impractical; a call for Mom always produced someone. But as the children grew up, conversations were confusing to the uninitiated, such as Eloise's husband. He found it all quite amusing, especially after they were married and Eloise, herself, became Mom ★

Life on the farm was peaceful, but there was always something to do. Eloise recalls the large threshing parties held when she was small. Neighbors went from farm to farm, helping each other with the work that had to be done. In 1961, Omar and Ruth decided to build a straw shed. The builder was the son and nephew of the Imhoff barn builders. Built into the long side of the barn, the shed created a third "end." The upper level of the structure was used to store straw, and cattle were provided first-floor shelter during the winter ★

Sanitation standards continued to change, and although Omar's barn was relatively new, it did not conform to the new regulations applied to dairy farms. Electing not to upgrade the barn, he sold his cows and, for the next few years, raised sheep and hogs. After Omar's death, in 1979, Ruth continued to live alone in the big farmhouse with help from her children ★

In 1988, the 160-acre farm was purchased by Scot Industries, which process and distribute steel tubing. The barn and land are leased to a farmer who grows corn and soybeans and keeps hogs in the barn. The dedication of Wayne County's Bicentennial Barn brought the whole Thorley family back to their former home. Eloise Snoddy, who lives just down the road, is pleased Scot Industries has taken such an interest in preserving the farm. She knows her ancestors would be honored to have their barn display Ohio's Bicentennial logo ★

OWNER
Melody and Philip Zuver

LOCATION
US Route 127, north of Bryan

The Williams County barn can be found a few miles north of Bryan, the county seat. Bryan was surveyed and laid out in 1840. It was named for John A. Bryan, a former state auditor, who donated the land for the formation of the town. The forests that once surrounded Bryan are gone. Huge trees were cut down to create farmland, their wood used to build barns and homes for the early settlers. Most of those buildings are gone, but still standing on a farm a few miles north of the city is a barn known as the Williams County Bicentennial Barn ★

The barn, now owned by Philip and Melody Zuver, was once part of a forty-acre plot purchased from the United States government by Isacc Perkins. Perkins added forty-five acres to complete his ninety-five-acre farm. It is believed that Lieutenant Colonel Thomas Clodfelter was responsible for building the distinctive brick house in 1865. Material to make the bricks came from the nearby creek bed ★

Franklin Elder, a veteran of the 3rd Ohio Cavalry, became the next owner of the farm. Elder started a brickyard on the farm, in continuous operation until 1892. Later the house became known as the Seven Pines Inn, so named because of seven, towering, pine trees that stand in the front yard ★

The barn on the property is estimated to be ninety years old. Built as a bank barn, it has an attached straw shed, with a mow on the upper level and an indoor yard below. Threshing took place on the upper floor, where there are two middle bays for that purpose and two outer bays for mow. With a bank two bays wide, the straw from the threshing machine could be blown into the straw shed mow through an inside door, and beyond through an outside door into the barnyard. According to Zuver, this would have required the threshman to set the threshing rig twice or in two different bays ★

And Zuver would know. He uses antique machinery to farm five of his nine acres. A ground-driven McCormick Deering grain binder and a 1935 Allis Chalmers WC tractor cut the grain. A 1920 Port Huron steam engine, provides power, while a Huber threshing machine, built in Marion, Ohio in the 1930s, separates the grain ★

Owner Philip Zuver threshing oats with his 1920 Port Huron steam engine. Courtesy of Melody and Philip Zuver.

Philip and Melody Zuver have only owned the farm for a few years. They are working on restoring the house, but do not plan to neglect the barn. Soon, it will receive new concrete approaches and retaining walls. The barn windows will have new trim along with flower boxes. Each year, the Zuvers hold a threshing day and use their antique equipment. In 2003, they will be threshing wheat and hope to have a larger event than in the past ★

Philip and Melody are pleased to be Bicentennial Barn owners. They were surprised when close to a hundred people arrived for the dedication. Melody and her mother and sister prepared food and invited family and friends to celebrate with them. The Zuvers hope the barn-painting project will interest children in the history of their state and in the agricultural traditions of farmers who settled Ohio 200 hundred years ago. They welcome you to the Williams County Bicentennial Barn ★

Wood

OWNER
Troy Cutchall

LOCATION
2416 State Route 163, east of Stony Ridge

The Wood County Bicentennial Barn was once part of a large farm in Lake Township. Visible from the Ohio Turnpike, the barn is a reminder of life before paved highways, when Wood County was part of the Black Swamp. In 1859, work began on 16,000 miles of drainage ditches, which turned the soggy earth into prime agricultural land. Little towns, with names like Latcha, sprang up at railroad stops, and farms flourished ★

The Petersen family maintained ownership of the farm for seventy-eight years. In 1876, county records show Ludwig Petersen purchased thirty acres, followed by a purchase of an adjoining ten acres in 1882. In 1924, Wood County conducted a Re-appraisement of Land. Reviewed in July of that year, the house on the property was listed as being thirty-five years old. The L-shaped barn was ten years old and recorded as having a Hip Roof and Plank Frame. The front section of the barn measured sixty by thirty-six feet and the rear section, fifty by thirty-six feet. Also noted were several outbuildings: a chicken coop, a tool house, and a granary ★

In 1940, the property transferred from Robert to Leonard Petersen. Mabel Petersen acquired it in 1946. In 1954, she sold the north portion of her property, as construction of the Ohio Turnpike bisected it ★

Wayne and Dorothy Warner owned eight acres of the former farm during the 1970s; they sold it to Henry and Carol Wasilausky in 1980. Troy Cutchall, the present owner, purchased it from Carol Wasilausky in December 1995. By then, all that remained of the original farm buildings were the house and barn ★

Cutchall, a construction worker, uses the barn for the storage of hay and straw but would like to find a more permanent use. Although in need of a roof and other repairs, the barn is structurally sound. He is exploring his options with the hope that he will be able to preserve it. He remains surprised at the interest generated by the barn-painting project and is pleased his barn represents Wood County ★

Wyandot

OWNER

Sam and Laura Ruffing

LOCATION

US Route 23, south of Carey

Sam Ruffing has fond memories of taking off across the fields, accompanied by his brother, to look for arrowheads. Long before Wyandot County was formed, the surrounding plains were favored grounds of the Wyandot Indians. The Indian relics were so plentiful that they surfaced after a rain and could always be found when the soil was turned ★

Over the years, the boys collected boxes of them. The habit of collecting things stayed with Sam. He continued to treasure items from the past and stored some in his father's old barn. The barn, which now belongs to Sam and his wife, Laura, proudly stands as the Wyandot County Bicentennial Barn ★

In 1948, when Sam was nine years old, his father, Charles Ruffing, bought the 76-acre farm. For Sam and his brother, moving to the farm was an adventure. The fields and surrounding countryside were theirs to enjoy. Charles worked at a job in the city, but somehow managed to find time to raise pigs, sheep, and a herd of dairy cows. Hay, fodder, and corn shucks were all stored in the haymow of the cavernous barn ★

Although he eventually bought a house in the city, Sam's heart never left the country. When his parents decided to sell the farm, Sam and Laura bought three acres of the property, including the house, barn, and outbuildings. The remaining acreage was sold to neighbors, who continue to farm it ★

Preserving old things has become somewhat of a hobby for Sam. Now retired, he brings home items found at garage sales and flea markets. Some he keeps, adding to his collections, others he buys to resell. He still has a box of arrowheads and other artifacts, reclaimed from the earth. Valued because of the storage it provides, the largest item he has attempted to preserve is his father's barn ★

Built in 1875, the barn has been well maintained. Sam had the siding painted in 1989, and the roof has been painted twice. Once used to shelter dairy cows, the barn now stores a tractor, some equipment, and Sam's "junk," as he calls it. The small shed, formerly a chicken coop, is also used for storage ★

Because of its age and proximity to the highway, the Ruffings' barn was an obvious choice to represent the county. Sam acknowledges that the Bicentennial Barn is an honor and a tribute to his father. Sam and Laura enjoy sharing the experience with their sixteen-year-old granddaughter, who lives with them. Perhaps, growing up with preservation-minded grandparents, she will develop an appreciation of the past and understand the value of preserving a part Ohio's farming tradition. That is, after all, what Bicentennial Barns are all about ★

With many thanks to . . .

JAMES BOGNAR AND JEANIE WATKO, for their unwavering friendship

WILLIAM LENDVAY, for his solicitous care of Spencer and Brownie

JENNIFER BUCCI, for the suggestion that started it all

DREW TEWKSBURY of Britton-Gallagher & Associates, Inc. in Solon

TODD JACKSON of Weston Hurd Fallon Paisley & Howley, L.L.P. in Cleveland

LAURA FREEMAN, for taking a chance on me

JUNE LUND SHIPLETT, for her encouragement

MOLLY RANDEL, for her support

PAT ZARLEY of the New Albany Plains Township Historical Society

JOYCE ALIG of the Mercer County Historical Society

MIKE SIBBERSON, Wood County Auditor

MARVIN MCKINLEY, Ashland County Historian

DIANA COY of the Paulding County Carnegie Library

CAROLYN STRALEY of Straley Real Estate in Paulding

Bibliography

Howe, Henry. *Historic Collections of Ohio*. Cincinnati: C.J. Krehbiel and Company. 1888.

Leffingwell, Randy. *The American Barn*. Osceola: MRI Publishing Company. 1997.

Noble, Allen G. and Richard K. Cleek. *The Old Barn Book*. New Brunswick: Rutgers Press. 1997.

Noble, Allen G. and Hubert G.H. Wilhelm. *Barns of the Midwest*. Athens: Ohio University Press. 1995.

Sommer, Robin Langley. *The Ultimate Book of Historic Barns*. San Diego: Thunder Bay Press. 2000.